BEYOND
THE GLASS

BEYOND
THE GLASS

a comprehensive guide to
WINDOW REPLACEMENT

Wisconsin Edition

SCOTT R YOUNG

Advantage®

Published by Advantage, Charleston, South Carolina.
Member of Advantage Media Group.

ADVANTAGE is a registered trademark and the Advantage colophon is a trademark of Advantage Media Group, Inc.

Printed in the United States of America.

ISBN: 978-159932-416-6
LCCN: 2014932579

This publication is designed to provide accurate and authoritative information in regard to the subject matter covered. It is sold with the understanding that the publisher is not engaged in rendering legal, accounting, or other professional services. If legal advice or other expert assistance is required, the services of a competent professional person should be sought.

Advantage Media Group is proud to be a part of the Tree Neutral® program. Tree Neutral offsets the number of trees consumed in the production and printing of this book by taking proactive steps such as planting trees in direct proportion to the number of trees used to print books. To learn more about Tree Neutral, please visit www.treeneutral.com. To learn more about Advantage's commitment to being a responsible steward of the environment, please visit www.advantagefamily.com/green

Advantage Media Group is a publisher of business, self-improvement, and professional development books and online learning. We help entrepreneurs, business leaders, and professionals share their Stories, Passion, and Knowledge to help others Learn & Grow. Do you have a manuscript or book idea that you would like us to consider for publishing? Please visit advantagefamily.com or call 1.866.775.1696.

ACKNOWLEDGMENTS

First and foremost I would like to thank my wife and best friend, Julie, for standing beside me over the past 32+ years. This book would not have been possible without her encouragement and support in both our personal and business lives.

I would like to thank my daughters Misty, Amber, Nicole and Erica for their support in critiquing the different parts of the book and inspiring me to be the best father I can be.

Thanks to my father and mother for bringing me up in a home with honesty, integrity and with the sound values that so many lack these days.

Thanks to my father, who believed in me from a very young age and taught me that using quality products and taking care of customers is the only way to succeed in business.

Thanks to my employees for everything I have learned in the past 30+ years and for their dedication in getting the job done right. I couldn't do it without them.

Thanks to the many organizations that have taught me so much about the home improvement industry over the years and how to run a successful business.

Without all of these people this book would not exist. To all, I am very grateful.

CONTENTS

INTRODUCTION

The typical homeowner doesn't know a lot about windows. That's why I wrote this book. I've been working with windows and doors for many years, and I hope to pass along what I've learned to help you make the most informed decisions possible when it's time to replace the windows in your home.

I grew up in the home improvement business that my father founded in the 1960s. When I took over the company in 1999, I decided to concentrate solely on production and installation of the highest quality windows and doors available. Today, AHT Wisconsin Windows, with locations in Clintonville, Madison, and the Fox Cities, is well known throughout the area for our superior products and customer service.

Something I learned from my father is that if you're going to do something, do it right. Don't try to rush through it. Don't settle for inferior materials. And don't try to do it yourself unless you have the right knowledge, skills, tools, and experience. Countless customers have chosen us because:

- they tried to replace their own windows and weren't happy with the results;

- they hired a general handyman to do the job and weren't happy with the results;

- they bought windows from a distributor that subcontracted installation, and they weren't happy with the results.

Ultimately, after they came to us, their stories all had happy endings. But think of all the headaches, time, resources, and money they could have saved if they just made the right choice in the first place. I hope to prevent some of the pitfalls that these folks encountered by educating you as to the simple steps to getting the job done right, whether you're replacing your own windows or having someone do it for you.

Happy reading, and happy window shopping!

CHAPTER ONE

DO YOU NEED TO REPLACE YOUR WINDOWS?

The short answer, probably, is yes.

"Now wait a minute," you're probably saying. "This guy's in the window business! Of course he's going to say I need new windows." Yes, I do own a window business, and yes, we're always happy to help new clients—but not at the expense of people who don't really need new windows. My point is this: most homeowners *would* benefit from replacing some or all of their windows, and in this chapter we'll discuss why.

IMPROVED ENERGY EFFICIENCY

The number-one reason homeowners replace windows is to improve energy efficiency. Windows typically comprise 10 to 25 percent of a home's exterior wall area and account for up to 50 percent of the home's heating and cooling needs, depending on the climate and the energy efficiency of the windows.[1] Of course homeowners want to get that percentage down as low as possible, both to reduce their own costs as well as to cut down on global energy consumption.

Many factors contribute to windows' energy efficiency—or inefficiency—and we're going to discuss them throughout this book. To start, however, let's look at the basics.

CONDUCTION

During the cold Wisconsin winters when it gets below zero, you just can't seem to get warm in your home no matter how high you set your heat, especially near the windows. You may even feel a draft when you walk by the windows. Conversely, in the summer, the air conditioner may be at the coolest setting, but it's still hot in the house.

Both situations are due to *conduction* (also referred to as *convection),* or the passage of heat or cold through surfaces—in this case the glass and window framing material. Some windows are more resistant to conduction than others because of their energy efficiency, as we'll discuss in the next chapter.

At this juncture, however, I should point out a major difference between most of the higher quality windows available today and the older windows still found in many homes: the number of glass layers comprising each window. Older windows were usually constructed with a single layer of glass, whereas newer windows are generally made up of double or triple layers. The number of layers is referred to as *glazing,* as in single-, double- or triple-*glazed* windows (You may also hear them called single-, double- or triple-*paned* windows.).

---

1   Energystar.gov

As you can imagine, increasing the number of surfaces significantly decreases conduction. Even so, you may still feel a breeze by your windows even if they are sealed properly. The air being conducted through the glass is generally hotter or colder than the air inside. The movement of the warmer air ascending and the cooler air descending creates the breeze-like sensation you may feel near the windows. This is especially noticeable in the winter when the cold is conducting through the windows. Depending on the rate of conduction, you may find fog, condensation, or even ice around your windows (usually at the bottom, since that's the coldest part).

During the winter months, condensation on window interiors can be an annoying issue for many homeowners in Wisconsin. Not only will it fog up your windows, but it can lead to much bigger problems like mold, mildew, and rotting window frames. Getting rid of problems before they do serious damage can save you a lot of headaches down the road.

Before we look at how to fix the issue, it helps to understand what causes window condensation in the first place. Window condensation happens when the warm air in your home comes in contact with a cold window. The window cools down the warm air, and because cold air can't hold as much moisture as warm air can, water vapor in the air gets pushed out, and condensation forms on the window, similar to when moisture condenses on the outside of a glass of ice water.

So what can you do to prevent condensation build-up on your windows? I've got a few tips:

1) **Wipe down your windows.** Although it won't stop moisture from getting on your windows, wiping down wet

windows will keep water from sitting, which will eventually lead to rot and mold.

2) **Use a dehumidifier.** So many things in your home can produce moisture to condensate on your windows. Taking a shower, drying a load of laundry, cooking dinner, and even breathing are all major sources of moisture in your home. Running a dehumidifier can greatly reduce the excess humidity in a room, and will help keep water off your windows.

3) **Ventilate better.** In addition to a dehumidifier, increasing the ventilation in your home can help keep your windows from getting fogged. Make sure to run fans regularly, and especially while cooking and showering. Keeping bathroom doors closed while bathing will help keep moisture from spreading to the rest of the house, and the bathroom window can be opened if needed. Also, a proper ventilation fan in the bathroom will help reduce the amount of moisture build-up in the air.

4) **Consider replacing your windows.** If your home has single-pane windows, fighting condensation will be a never-ending battle. The piece of glass being chilled by ice-cold Wisconsin weather is the same piece of glass meeting the warm interior of your home. Because of this, moisture will build up despite all of your efforts. Double-paned glass is, of course, better than single-paned, but depending on how cold it is outside, you will still have condensation issues. And, of course, if you add the third layer of glass, it takes significantly longer for the condensation to occur. In addition, you can also add a gas that is denser than air

to slow down conduction even more. This will also help reduce condensation from forming on your windows. We'll talk more about these types of gases in the next chapter.

Something you might want to consider each autumn as you're putting the storm windows up (and again each spring as you're taking them down), is that the double- and triple-glazed windows on the market today are significantly more energy efficient *alone* than older single-glazed windows with storm windows attached. With technology today there is no need for storm windows at all.

AIR INFILTRATION

Another way air passes from outside to inside the home is through cracks and gaps in the window frames and/or sashes. This is known as *air infiltration,* which is usually due to:

- windows that are not properly installed
- sloppy framing, caulking, or weather-stripping around the window
- faulty sealing of the glass to the window frame or sash
- shrinkage of framing materials due to aging and weather conditions, particularly in vinyl and wood windows
- the sun cracking and drying out glazing material (the putty holding the glass in the window)
- broken or cracked glass

Higher energy costs, increased noise from outside, rattling, and difficulty opening and closing the windows can all result from poor window sealing. Plus, it can just look bad! Dirty or cracked old caulking, shoddy carpentry, mold, mildew, rotted wood, or the addition of plastic or tape in hopes of reducing airflow can certainly detract from a home's appearance.

EASE OF OPERATION AND MAINTENANCE

Ease of operation and maintenance—particularly cleaning—is the second most frequent reason homeowners replace their windows. Most newer windows either swing, slide, or tilt in for easier cleaning, meaning you no longer have to go outside to wash the exterior surfaces—you can wash them from inside the house.

Replacement windows available today are generally much easier and safer to maintain and operate than older windows. Simply opening and closing some older windows can be difficult or even impossible, due to swelling, painting, damaged or inoperable balance systems, worn out hardware, faulty locks, missing handles, and countless other problems.

Such operational problems can be extremely annoying and even dangerous. For example, if you can't open your windows, let's hope you never have a fire in your house. If you're propping a window open with a stick, a book, or some other object, let's hope a child (or anyone else) doesn't knock it out, causing the window to slam shut on their fingers.

SECURITY, SOUND, AND OTHER FACTORS

Many older windows don't have locks, and even if they do, they may not work very well. This can pose major security concerns as well as safety issues. Windows today come with a variety of locking mechanisms, and additional security hardware can be added as needed—in homes where small children live or visit frequently, for example, or homes in higher-crime neighborhoods.

Another reason homeowners replace old windows is excessive street or neighborhood noise. Not only do triple-glazed windows cut down on conduction, but they also reduce sound transmission and can help curtail unwanted noise much better than double-glazed windows do.

When Do You Need New Windows?

- Your home is cold in the winter and hot in the summer no matter how high you set the heat or air conditioning.

- Your monthly energy bills keep going up.

- In the winter you feel a chill every time you walk past a window.

- You feel a cold draft from the window while trying to relax in your easy chair.

- The glass in your windows ices over, or rattles in the wind.

- Evidence of seal failure: dirt or moisture trapped between the panes of glass.

- Mold or mildew has formed around your window frames.

- The curtains billow and blow even when the windows are closed.

- Your windows are difficult to open or close.

- Your windows don't lock or unlock properly.

- You have to go outside to clean your exterior window surfaces.
- You have plastic on your windows.
- You have storm windows.
- You want to increase the value of your home.
- Your windows are an eyesore.

KEEP IN MIND:

- Excessive moisture in your home can come from ordinary household activities, such as washing clothes, showering, keeping a fish tank, and so on.
- Air infiltration can cause you to lose heated or cooled air, leading to higher fuel bills.
- An unlocked window is an invitation to a burglar. Home security is an important function of a well-designed window.
- Conduction can be as bad or worse than air infiltration in causing high heating or cooling bills.

There are a multitude of other reasons for homeowners to replace windows—including the obvious "it's broken." Remodeling, aesthetics, increasing a home's value and "curb appeal," are some other factors that come into play. But as we discussed at the beginning of the chapter, the first and foremost reason is to improve energy efficiency, which we'll discuss even further in Chapter 2.

CHAPTER TWO

ENERGY EFFICIENCY AND GLASS QUALITY

I n this chapter we'll look at many of the different features available in today's windows, with an emphasis on the factors with the most impact on energy efficiency. Windows almost always represent the largest source of unwanted heat loss and heat gain in buildings.[2] In locales with extreme weather conditions like those we have here in Wisconsin, the importance of minimizing heat loss in the winter and heat gain in the summer should not be underestimated. Window quality can make a huge difference in energy costs and home value—not to mention plain old year-round comfort.

The quality and variety of windows has increased greatly over the last 15 to 20 years. That's not to say that subpar windows aren't still available—they most certainly are—but generally the quality is much higher, and that's primarily due to advances in technology and engineering in the glass-manufacturing industry.

---

2   Environmental Protection Agency (EPA), Energy Star Buildings Manual

When shopping for replacement windows you'll be inundated with all kinds of numbers and ratings and terms you may not be familiar with. This is due in large part to the sheer complexity of window production today. At one time it may have been true that "a window is a window is a window," but that is not the case anymore.

There's even a fancy name for the glass in windows: IGUs, or insulated glass units. An IGU refers to the glass portion of a window, including the spacer system and multiple layers of glass with very dry air or inert gas between the layers. The entire unit is then hermetically sealed, eliminating possible condensation between the glass and providing superior insulating properties (see cross-section below).

There are several factors relating to glass that you should keep in mind when shopping for window replacements:

- How many layers of glass does the window contain?

- How thick is the IGU (insulated glass unit)? Remember the thicker it is, the more insulating value you receive.

- How much air space is between each layer?

- What fills the space between the layers?

- What is the spacer system made of and how is it sealed?

- What type of low-e glass and how many layers are added to the unit?

Each of these factors plays a significant role in a window's energy efficiency.

LAYERS OF GLASS (AND GAS)

As we discussed briefly in the previous chapter, there are single-, double-, and triple-glazed windows on the market today. Each layer typically adds cost. So, as a rule, single-glazed windows are the least expensive to buy, and triple-glazed are the most expensive to buy.

SINGLE-GLAZED

Especially in a climate like that of Wisconsin, I would never recommend single-glazed windows as replacements. The purchase cost may be low, but so is the energy efficiency. You might as well throw your money *out* the window! Seriously, any single-glazed window you might use as a replacement wouldn't offer much, if any, improvement over the window currently in place. I would strongly urge you not to waste your time or money on single-glazed window replacements.

DOUBLE-GLAZED

Some of the ready-made, or stock, windows you'll find at lumber-yards or large home-supply stores are double-glazed IGUs with varying degrees of energy efficiency, based on several factors we'll discuss in a minute.

TRIPLE-GLAZED

Popular throughout Canada and northern Europe, triple-glazed windows are becoming increasingly common across the colder areas of the United States. Triple glazing is provided through a third layer—either a third sheet of glass between the two outside panes or, less commonly, a plastic film suspended between the two panes of glass.

GLASS THICKNESS

The thickness of the glass makes a huge difference, also. When someone refers to ½-inch IGUs, it doesn't mean that the glass itself is ½-inch thick. It means that you've got two sheets of glass that are each 1/8-inch thick, with ¼-inch of air space between them. The overall measurement, from outside surface to outside surface, is ½ inch— the typical width for double-glazed windows. Triple-glazed windows are generally 1 inch thick, and made of three sheets of glass. They are also much more energy efficient than single or double glazed glass.

AMOUNT OF AIR SPACE

Increasing the amount of air space between the sheets of glass makes the IGU more energy efficient. If the air space gets too wide, however, convection loops form, increasing convective heat loss through the window. A balance of all the efficiencies and thorough testing is the only way to make sure you have the most energy efficient IGU possible for your climate. We'll discuss this in more depth later in the book.

LOW-CONDUCTIVITY GAS FILL

Because heat or cold conduction across the air space in a sealed IGU contributes to heat loss or gain, performance is improved by replacing the air with a lower-conductivity gas. The most commonly used gas fill is argon, which is plentiful, inexpensive, and inert. More effective gases such as krypton slow down conductivity even more and can be found in the highest-performing windows. You may also see IGUs that use something called trigon as a filler, which is a mixture of argon, krypton, and air. As you would expect, the energy efficiency of trigon is less than that of pure krypton but more than that of pure argon.

To compare the effectiveness of the gases, we use this analogy: If you're running through air, there's a little resistance, but not much. So if the space in the IGU is filled with air (rather than with krypton or argon), it's like running through air. Using the same analogy, if you were running through argon, it would be like running in a swimming pool. It slows you down; you can't run as fast because there's a lot of resistance. Krypton, however, creates even more resistance. It would be like running through peanut butter. Of the three, krypton does the best job of slowing conduction through the IGU.

LOW-EMISSIVITY COATINGS

First introduced in the late 1970s, low-e (low emissivity glass) has grown tremendously in popularity. A thin transparent coating of silver or tin oxide on the glass surface, allows short-wavelength sunlight to pass through but blocks long-wavelength heat radiation. Low-e coating also helps protect against fading of carpet, fabrics, paper, artwork, paints, and wood by reducing the amount of ultra-violet (UV) rays passing through windows.

Low-e coatings are not one-size-fits-all: both the type and the placement of these coatings contribute to wide variations in performance metrics. Windows manufactured for use in cold climates are coated with a different low-e formula than those manufactured for warmer climates. In Wisconsin, for example, we want the benefit of solar heat gain in the winter, but we want to reflect that heat in the summer. The right low-e coatings can make all the difference in how comfortable you are in your home.

I had clients who had their dining room table next to a big picture window. They couldn't even use that table when the sun was out, because the sun's heat simply baked them. When we replaced that window with one that had low-e glass, they could use that space any time in comfort because most of the heat was now being reflected outside. It's nice to hear from my customers that our windows have let them reclaim a part of their house that the weather had made them abandon, and that's something we hear quite often.

If you want to do a simple test of your own windows' energy efficiency, get a 250-watt heat lamp, plug it in and send someone outside with it. Have them hold it near the window outside, and put your hand to the glass on the inside. The more heat you feel coming through, the less energy efficient the glass is.

WARM-EDGE GLAZING SPACERS

Insulated glass units are sealed around the perimeter by spacers that maintain the distance between the sheets of glass and help seal in any gas fills being used. Aluminum has been the most common material for glazing spacers, but it is very thermally conductive. *Warm-edge spacers* using rubber, foam, silicone, thermally broken steel, and other materials have become common in windows, and drastically reduce heat loss or gain at the edges of IGUs. Years ago it was common for people to brag about how energy efficient their glass was. However, they only tested it at the center of glass. The least energy efficient part of the glass is the edge. In winter, as you go from center of glass to the edge, you will find that it becomes colder. The right spacer system in this situation makes all the difference. That's where the term "warm edge technology" comes from.

PERFORMANCE METRICS

Heat loss through windows, solar heat gain during heating periods, and avoidance of solar gain during cooling periods should all factor into window selection. To enable apples-to-apples comparisons among windows, industry leaders formed the National Fenestration Rating Council (NFRC) in 1989 to create standard metrics for comparing performance in windows.[3]

ENERGY PERFORMANCE RATINGS	
U-Factor (U.S./I-P)	Solar Heat Gain Coefficient
0.16	0.26
ADDITIONAL PERFORMANCE RATINGS	
Visible Transmittance	Air Leakage (U.S./I-P)
0.41	0.10

As you can see on the sample window label above, there are several standard categories in which window performance is rated.

The U-factor is the rate at which a window conducts nonsolar heat flow. It is usually expressed in units of BTU/hr-ft2-oF. NFRC U-factor ratings represent the entire window performance, including glazing, frame, and spacer material. *The lower the U-factor, the more energy efficient the window.*

Solar heat gain coefficient (SHGC) is the fraction of solar radiation admitted through a window—either transmitted directly and/or absorbed—and subsequently released as heat inside a home. The lower the SHGC, the less solar heat it transmits and the greater its shading ability. *A product with a high SHGC rating is more effective at collecting solar heat during the winter.* A product with a low SHGC rating is more effective at reducing cooling loads during the summer

---

3   buildinggreen.com

by blocking heat gain from the sun. Your home's climate, orientation, and external shading will determine the optimal SHGC for a particular window. In Wisconsin it is important to note that winter is when we want the most solar heat gain. Again, a balance of all the window technologies out there and consideration of your particular climate are all factors to be considered for optimal performance.

Air leakage is the rate of air movement around a window in the presence of a specific pressure difference across it. A product with a low air-leakage rating is tighter than one with a high air-leakage rating. Now, in English: This is what causes your drapes and curtains to move, and the air you can feel coming in through cracks and gaps around the window sash and frame when the wind is blowing. Essentially, the window is not blocking the force of the air from infiltrating the inside of your home.

Visible transmittance (VT) measures how much natural light the window allows into your room. The higher the number, the more natural light can get through.

R-value refers to the resistance of the window to heat conduction, and it is the inverse of the U-factor (that is, R-value = 1/U-factor). Better windows have high R-values and low U-factors (This energy performance rating isn't always provided.) Keep in mind that the R-value could be for a particular part of a window; the glass, frame material, and so on. However, the U-factor is a compilation of the energy efficiency of the whole window unit and is a better indicator of how well an entire window unit will perform.

WHAT IS ENERGY STAR?

The Energy Star rating was established by the EPA in 1992. It is a voluntary program that identifies and promotes energy efficient products and buildings to reduce energy consumption, improve energy security, and reduce pollution through voluntary labeling of or other forms of communication about products and buildings that meet the highest energy efficiency standards.

To earn the label, Energy Star products must be third-party certified based on testing in EPA-recognized laboratories. In addition to up-front testing, a percentage of all Energy Star products are subject to "off-the-shelf" verification testing each year. The goal of this testing is to ensure that changes or variations in the manufacturing process do not undermine a product's qualification with Energy Star requirements.

PUT TO THE TEST

I've included the results of a study conducted by the University of Illinois that does a good job of demonstrating the energy efficiency— or lack thereof—of various types of windows. For the study, a "room within a room" was constructed. The temperature of the "outside" room was maintained at 0 degrees (Fahrenheit), and the temperature of the "inside" room was set at 68 degrees. Much like a house, the "inside room" had windows installed around the perimeter. The windows were all the same size, but different in terms of glazing, glass thickness, gas filling, coating, and so on (see image, based on this study, below).

UNIVERSITY OF ILLINOIS COMPARES GLASS INSIDE TEMPERATURES

ROOM WITHIN A ROOM

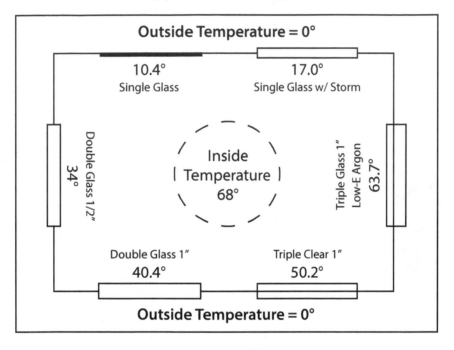

As you can see, the differences between the windows made a dramatic impact on how energy efficient each window was, as measured by the inside glass temperature of each window. Obviously, in this room you would want to be next to the tripled-glazed window with low-e coating and argon filling (and keep in mind that krypton filling would have slowed down conduction even more, but wasn't available when this testing was performed).

If you're on the fence about double-glazed versus triple-glazed IGUs, or whether to go with argon-filled rather than krypton-filled IGUs, take a look at this glass efficiency comparison (see image below).

GLASS EFFICIENCY COMPARISON

	Ordinary Dual Glazed clear/clear	Ordinary Dual Glazed LowE/clear	Dual Glazed LowE/clear Argon	Triple Glazed LowE/clear/ LowE Argon	Triple Glazed LowE2/ clear/LowE2 Krypton
U Value (lower the number the better)	0.48	0.31	0.26	0.19	0.11
R Value (higher the number the better)	2.08	3.23	3.85	5.26	9.09
Solar Heat Gain Coefficient (total window) SHGC	0.78	0.41	0.30	0.28	0.25

Look at the difference! Don't believe anyone who tries to tell you that triple-glazing and krypton filling doesn't make much of an impact on the energy efficiency of windows. Granted, the level of performance they provide might be overkill in milder climates. But in weather like we have here in Wisconsin, their superior performance generally pays for itself in energy savings more quickly than you might think.

KEEP IN MIND:

• Triple-paned windows offer the maximum efficiency.

- The thicker the Insulated Glass Unit, the more insulating value you receive.

- On a window's rating sticker, the lower the U-factor, the better the window will perform in saving energy.

CHAPTER THREE

WINDOW STYLES, MATERIALS, AND CONSTRUCTION

When we go into somebody's home, we'll initially do a window inspection on each of the windows in their home, figure out what the issues are, and then we ask them, if you could have any type window you wanted, what would it be? Often their answers are based on the problems they've had with the current windows; "I've got these crank-outs, and when we want to close them, one of us has to go outside and push it shut and the other one's got to lock it. So we don't want anything like that." But of course, with a 50-year nonprorated warranty on the new crank windows, that's not going to be a problem with new windows, so our questions are really directed to the style of window they prefer.

The kind of window you choose has to work esthetically with the space it's going into. And there's a ton of options: You can even make the window bigger or smaller. In a house we worked on recently, the owner was removing his old siding and altering the openings to fit a different size of window from those he'd had previously. Obviously, that's an additional expense, but one that some people are willing to take on in order to get what they really want. Our main business is making a custom-built window that fits the opening that's there, but it's good to know that you're not locked into that particular size and type.

Just as homes are built in many different styles and with many different types of materials, so are windows. In this chapter we'll talk about the pros and cons of the most common window styles and materials available today.

SINGLE-HUNG WINDOWS

On a single-hung window, only the bottom sash slides upward—the top sash is permanently fixed. On single-hung tilt windows, the bottom sash tilts inward to enable cleaning of the exterior face. Cleaning the exterior of the top face, however, must be done outside or by trying to reach it from inside, which can be difficult if not impossible.

Single-hung windows typically cost less than other window styles (because the top sash doesn't need a balance system) and often aren't available in high-performance models.

Pros:

- Low cost

Cons:

- Low performance

- Top sash is difficult or impossible to clean from inside.

- Usually lacks any energy efficiency

- The windows in your home now are probably as good and maybe better than a single hung window.

DOUBLE-HUNG WINDOWS

Both the top and bottom sashes open on a double-hung window. On double-hung tilt windows, the sashes tilt inward to enable easy cleaning of the exterior faces of both the top and bottom sash.

Since double-hung windows open without using any interior or exterior space, they're an excellent choice for small rooms or next to walkways, porches, or patios, where you don't want a window to protrude.

Most new double-hung windows use spring balances to support the sashes, but traditionally, counterweights held in boxes on either side of the window were used. These were attached to the sashes using pulleys of either braided cord or, later, purpose-made chain.

Pros:

- Good for small rooms or areas where you don't want a protrusion from the wall
- Traditional styling matches many older homes
- Convenient cleaning (tilt-in models)

Cons:

- Depending on frame material, can be difficult to open and close due to swelling

CASEMENT WINDOWS

A casement window is hinged at the side and opens outward. It provides excellent ventilation—at times literally reaching out and catching the breeze. It looks like a narrow picture window because, unlike double hung or sliding windows, it has no rail to obstruct the view.

Some casement windows are simply pushed open, but most

have a hand crank. If you're installing windows over a sink, counter-top, or appliance, a casement window with a crank can be the perfect solution (presuming that you can reach the crank handle to open it).

Of all the window styles that open, casement windows generally allow the least amount of air leakage—provided they are installed correctly.

Pros:

- good ventilation

- ease of operation

- less air leakage than other styles (if installed properly)

Cons:

- Casement windows will protrude out onto patios and walkways and may create a hazard of people walking into them. Caution must be exercised when choosing a casement in these situations.

AWNING WINDOWS

An awning window is hinged at the top and opens outward. Opened outward, the glass protects the opening like an awning, enabling ventilation even during rainy weather.

Awning windows are often used for basements because they can be placed high on the wall to let in both light and air. In many cases they are also placed under picture windows to provide ventilation.

Pros:

- Awning windows fit in small areas.
- They can be used for ventilation in rainy weather.

Cons:

- They are difficult to clean exterior surface of outward-opening models.

SLIDER WINDOWS

Single slider windows have one side that slides open, whereas both sashes slide in double sliders. In a pocket slider they'll both slide, but don't hinge open; you have to lift them up and pull them in for cleaning. "Tilt and slide" windows, which both pivot and slide, allow for easy cleaning of both internal and external surfaces from inside the home.

Fair warning, however: Other than top-of-the-line slider windows like ours, this is the style we see the most problems with in terms of air leakage, cleaning difficulties, and generally poor construction.

Pros:

- Maximum sizes can be larger than an awning or casement window.

Cons:

- air leakage
- difficult operation and cleaning (some models)

BAY AND BOW WINDOWS

bay window

bow window

A bay window is a combination of typically three windows that dramatically extend from your home.

A bow window is very similar to a bay window, except it is composed of four or more windows joined at equal angles to form a more even curve.

Bay and bow windows give your home a custom designer look and feel, plus add extra space and dimension to any room without the expense of traditional room expansions.

Pros:

- Bay and bow windows increase value and "curb appeal" of home.

- They add space and focal point to a room.

- They add an area for displaying favorite things including plants and knickknacks.

Cons:

- Because of the value and curb appeal they add to a home, there are no real cons.

WINDOW GRILLES

You may have noticed in the photos that some windows have bars dividing the glass into smaller, decorative windowpanes. Historically, true divided-light windows were made up of individually glazed panes of glass within the grilles, or *muntins*—a very inefficient design that's prone to drafts. Most window manufacturers today offer grille options that provide the look of divided light but are more energy efficient. Some grilles are mounted outside the glass for a more authentic, period look; others are placed between the layers of glass. One thing to remember here is that if they are installed outside the glass, the window becomes harder to clean than if they are located between the glass layers.

WINDOW FRAME MATERIALS

The material of a window's frame has a significant bearing on an insulated window's price, appearance, and durability. It also has a major impact on the thermal characteristics of the window. A window's U-factor incorporates the thermal properties of both the frame and the glazing. Since the sash and frame represent from 10 to 30 percent of the total area of the window unit, the frame properties significantly influence the total window performance.[4]

---

4   U.S. Department of Energy, Efficient Windows Collaborative

The materials most often used are wood, aluminum, vinyl, fiberglass, and composites made from a mixture of resins and polymers chosen for superior strength, insulation, and durability. Let's talk a little about each.

WOOD

Well-constructed, wood window frames insulate relatively well, but also swell in Wisconsin summer weather, which can lead to difficultly in operation. When they shrink, as in the wintertime when it's drier, they can allow more air infiltration. Upkeep is the primary downside to wood frames, as they require frequent sealing, staining, or painting. Wood window frames are also prone to rot, which weakens them and makes it difficult for them to hold paint.

A variation of the wood-framed window is to clad the exterior face of the frame with either vinyl or aluminum, creating a weather-resistant surface. Clad frames have lower maintenance requirements, while retaining the attractive wood finish on the interior. However, if they're not sealed properly between the cladding and the wood, they can allow the wood to rot out, unseen, beneath the cladding.

ALUMINUM

Aluminum window frames are lightweight, strong, durable, and easily extruded into the complex shapes required for window parts. Aluminum frames are available in anodized and factory-baked enamel finishes that are relatively durable and low-maintenance.

The biggest disadvantage of aluminum as a window frame material is its high thermal conductance. It readily conducts heat and cold, greatly raising the overall U-factor of a window unit. In cold climates, a simple aluminum frame can easily become cold enough to condense moisture, frost or even ice on the inside surfaces of window frames. We have all been in a hotel in the winter and have noticed the windows that are made with aluminum frames are frosted and iced up, sometimes over half way to the top. My advice to you is: aluminum is not an insulator and, given Wisconsin weather, should be avoided.

VINYL

Vinyl window frames are usually made of polyvinyl chloride (PVC) with ultraviolet light (UV) stabilizers to keep sunlight from breaking down the material as much as possible. There are differences in the quality of one manufacturer's vinyl compared to another. This is because a vinyl window frame is made from a compound—a recipe of sorts—that dictates its performance over time. Each additive to a company's vinyl recipe helps determine the long-term characteristics of the final product, like its weatherability and impact resistance.

Topping the list of vinyl's advantages are its low cost and minimal maintenance requirements. Vinyl windows generally do not need painting, although some consumers complain about warping, cracking, fading, and yellowing that occur over time. Another downside is their aesthetics, which many people consider inferior.

A third major drawback is vinyl's very high coefficient of thermal expansion. Over time, expansion and contraction from temperature changes can loosen seals and cause cracks at corners and on flanges, significantly reducing energy efficiency.

FIBERGLASS

Fiberglass windows have come and gone over the years. Reputable manufacturers tried in the past to make a fiberglass window that would work dependably, but nobody's ever successfully made one that could withstand our Wisconsin weather. Some manufacturers are dipping their toes back into the fiberglass window market but, again, you're talking about a product with no record of success and no track record, so it's impossible to assess the value of their warranty.

The first big problem with these windows is the resin smell they emit. To put it bluntly, fiberglass resin stinks. It continues to do so after they're in your home, so your whole home smells of fiberglass resin for quite a while. The other, bigger issue is their durability. Fiberglass windows can't be fusion welded, so manufacturers have to glue the corners and the miters together. Inevitably, the glue fails and the windows end up falling apart. For these reasons, fiberglass windows aren't popular with consumers, who are justifiably wary of using an unproven product.

COMPOSITE

Composite windows can mean a variety of different things to different manufacturers, but generally come in two basic types:

- Wood composites, which combine chemically-bonded blends of wood with plastic resins for a frame that looks wood-like, but doesn't require as much maintenance as wood.

- Resin/polymer composites, which combine resin, chemical additives, and modifiers for superior strength, durability, and energy efficiency. As an example, some composite frames are as much as 60 percent more energy efficient than wood and 200 percent more energy efficient than vinyl.

Composite window frames vary from manufacturer to manufacturer, but are typically a great deal stronger than vinyl frames and more resistant to moisture and expansion/contraction in varying weather conditions. In addition, composite frames are virtually maintenance-free. A wide selection of colors and finishes are available, including interior wood-grain laminates to simulate a true wood window. We're starting to see more and more composite frames used in the highest-performance windows. This makes sense, because if you're making an investment in top-of-the-line glass and gas filler, you want to "house" it in the best possible frame, which in many cases is made from a composite material.

WINDOW FRAME CONSTRUCTION

Many window frames and sashes are held together with staples or screws and caulk that can loosen or weaken over time. These are referred to as *mechanically fastened* frames. The alternative is *fusion-welded* frames, in which the frame material is heated until soft enough for the pieces to join together as one. Even if mechanically fastened frames are caulked at the joints, welded frames are considerably more energy efficient, water tight and more durable.

KEEP IN MIND:

- There are a wide variety of designs and window types available to suit any style of home. What you choose depends on your tastes and the functionality of the window in the space where it's to be used.

- You CAN choose larger windows when you're having new ones installed, although it will require additional work on your home to fit them.

- Well-made composite windows are the most durable and reliable.

CHAPTER FOUR

STOCK VERSUS CUSTOM-MADE WINDOWS

Imagine you're a homeowner, looking to replace a window with a premanufactured stock window. You measure the width and the height of your current window, and then you go down to the local lumberyard or big box home improvement store and find a window there that's as close to the measurements as you can get.

If the window you choose is slightly wider than the one you're replacing, you're going to have to do some fairly involved structural work on your house to make it fit. If it's narrower, if you're two or three inches or four inches off in width or height, now you've got to fill it in a couple inches on each side. Additionally, the casing that's inside your home has to be redone along with the siding on the outside, because now you have a wider gap. The fact is this is a situation in which "close enough" really isn't; you have to get the width and the height *exactly right*—and it's just about impossible to do that with a stock window. Houses shift and settle over time too, which further complicates getting the fit right.

With a custom-built window, that's not a problem. Typically, when we're asked to do a window replacement, we go in and measure the exact opening and can make a window exactly the right size to fit the opening that's there. People have beautiful woodwork inside their home and do not want it disturbed, so they get to keep the same woodwork and they don't have any siding problems on the outside.

When you take a stock window that's not exactly right, and you have to build it in, it takes longer, requires far more labor, and takes more material. These things all add additional cost in fill-in material as well as more labor. Typically, by the time you buy a stock window and have somebody install it, you could have had a custom-made window installed for less or the same price, because you don't have all that labor time. Because it's a perfect fit, it doesn't take long to put them in, not to mention it will look far better because it was made to fit your home.

Instead of paying for labor, try to purchase the most window you can get for your investment dollar. Custom-made windows are easier to install and require fewer modifications, if any, so you can purchase a higher quality window. As an example, I've seen the labor savings actually save enough for the homeowners to get triple-glazed IGUs instead of having to settle for double-glazed.

There are other potential hazards of buying a stock window and having it installed by a carpenter or handyman. Say you choose to buy your new stock windows at a home store, and then hire somebody to do the installation. He puts the windows in, making the adjustments for that inch or two difference between your house's openings and the stock window sizes, and they look just fine. Then, one day, you're trying to crank one open and it doesn't open, because for some reason it's stuck at one of the corners. You call your installer back and say, "Hey, one of my windows isn't working. Come check it out." He comes out, looks at it and says, "That's not my problem.

The window sash is sagging because the manufacturer didn't make it right. Let me get ahold of them for you." He calls them, and tells you, "They're going to be in the area about a month from now, on a Tuesday. You'll need to be there to show them the window." Now you've got to take part of a day off work to meet the representative. The window manufacturer's representative shows up, looks at it, and says, "No, that's definitely not our problem. It was put in wrong. It was supposed to be nailed like this and it's nailed like that. Therefore it's not our responsibility; it's the guy that put it in."

In short, what you get is the runaround, because nobody wants to take responsibility for what's going on in your home. The manufacturing company is not going to honor the warranty, because it claims it's the contractor's fault. The contractor says it's a problem with the window so he's not going to fix it. Guess who loses? And this presumes that your original contractor is even willing to show up and inspect your stuck window. We see a whole lot more contractors who aren't willing to go that distance than those who are.

Let's just say a year after you put them in, something goes wrong and you try to call the contractor who did it, but you don't get an answer, or the phone is out of service because he's out of business. Now, as far as the contractor is concerned, you don't have anybody to take care of it. You say to yourself, "Well, I know who manufactured the window," so you Google the manufacturer's name, find the company's 800 number to call, and the sales rep comes out. It's the same situation: he tells you the same thing, and you're still stuck with a window that doesn't work properly.

Unfortunately in these situations, the burden's always on the consumer to fix a problem when shoddy people do the work. Typically, it's the work that's at fault; less often, it's the manufacturer. The manufacturers and contractors can point the finger at one another and all you get is the run around.

That's not a business model that a responsible professional follows. Our company, for example, takes complete responsibility for the work we do and the products we provide. We sell you the window, we install the window, and we service the window. If you have any problems, you call us and we take care of it. If it's a manufacturer defect, we contact the manufacturer, we get the new part or piece or whatever's required, and we fix it—period. We've been in business since 1967 doing what we do, so we know exactly what it is and we can get it fixed for you. There's no cost to you, and no runaround.

My father always told me that it's not the problem that matters. It's what you *do* about the problem that matters.

The other situation we see too often in the home improvement industry is when contractors agree to do a job yet seem totally disinterested in finishing the job once they've started. Typically, they'll start a project, and then they'll take off for a week and go to somebody else's project and work on that, because that guy started screaming because the contractor wasn't showing up there. Then they'll come back and work a day or two on your project. Then, when someone else starts screaming, they'll be gone again. Sometimes it's weeks and weeks or months before they actually finish it. This isn't something that you, as a consumer, should ever have to put up with.

Years and years ago, when my father owned the company, we decided that once we contract for a job and we're on that job working, we are not pulling off of that job until it's complete. Once it's done to the customer's satisfaction, only then do we go on to the next job and complete that project. People ask us, "Well, when can you get it done? We want it done right away," and I tell them,

"We have a four- to six-week backlog right now, but when we come to do your project, we're going to be here until the project's done. The person's whose project we're working on while you're waiting for yours gets that same consideration. When we're done, you're going to have everything you've contracted for and the job will be complete before we go to the next person." I believe in the long run people appreciate this type of service versus working for a few days, pulling off the job, and letting people wonder when you're going to complete it. I also believe you get a better job when everything is organized and complete.

Another important factor to consider in weighing the relative value of custom versus stock windows for most people is whether the window is **Energy Star** certified or not and if it has NFRC certification. Without those certifications, it's certainly not suitable for the kind of weather we have in Wisconsin, because of the heat we have here in the summer and the extreme cold in the winter. Once you look at that, you want to be certain that your contractor doesn't just slide under the radar with **Energy Star** ratings and NFRC ratings; you need to make sure your window is very energy efficient.

As we discussed earlier, in judging the window's energy efficiency, the first thing to look for is the glass. There's double glass and triple glass. There's double glass with smaller spaces in between the glass and then there are double panes with bigger spaces in between the glass. The bigger the space between the glass, the more energy efficient it is. Then we have triple-pane glass with smaller and bigger spaces between the glass. Again, the bigger the space between the glass, the more energy efficient it is. Despite being the most efficient, triple-pane windows aren't sold at home stores. One major manufacturer advertises a triple-pane window, but it's really just a double-pane with a storm window on it. It's not actually a hermetically sealed, triple-pane IGU (insulated glass unit), although it's nominally better than a double-pane.

There are other valuable features that a custom-made window offers that simply aren't available with a stock, home-store window. You won't get double low-E on a big box store window. You may not get two locks; sometimes the width of a double-hung window dictates how many locks the manufacturer puts on it. A lot of companies produce a three-foot-wide window with one lock on it, which simply is not going to provide any real security. Even the balance system put in the window will be the cheapest one, versus something that's going to last.

You won't get a decent warranty, despite the overuse of the buzzword "lifetime warranty." At every box store you go to, they'll say, "Well, it's a lifetime warranty, lifetime warranty, lifetime warranty," but rather than depend on what you're told, you need to get a copy of that warranty and read it. Usually, you'll discover there's a proration schedule. After the first year, they'll cover 100 percent. A lock breaks, let's say, and they'll cover 100 percent of it as far as material's are concerned. It doesn't have anything to do with labor; they'll simply send you a new lock. By the time 10 years is up, you'll pay 90 percent for that lock and they'll pay 10 percent. Then it'll stay like that for the "lifetime." You should also be aware that according to the Bureau of Consumer Protection here in Wisconsin, the word "lifetime" used in a window warranty is very vague. Here is the definition they gave us when we asked them about a "lifetime" warranty:

If a window comes with a lifetime warranty the question is whose or what's lifetime—the lifetime of the company that manufactured the window, the lifetime of the installer, the lifetime of the purchaser, the lifetime of the window?

As you can probably imagine when it comes time to honor the warranty there will be many ways for the warranty to be interpreted. The buzz word "lifetime warranty" is just that, it really only feels good to hear it before you purchase something and very rarely covers anything significant when something does go wrong with the product. Most people find this out after it is too late.

Even new construction isn't as good in this respect as it ought to be. Here's what builders do: They find out what people want and they find out what their budget is and then they try to pack everything in the budget they can. All the "wants," the bells and whistles, get stuck into the quote before the quality is figured into windows, siding, roof, and the rest of the basics. Those are the things they skimp on. If people want a Jacuzzi instead of nice windows, the builders would rather get that Jacuzzi installed because it makes people happier than energy-efficient windows. Then, 10 years later (or in some cases, from day one), when those windows aren't operating properly and they're letting cold air in, those same folks have to spend the extra money to replace them and have quality windows installed.

I know this from my own experience. I tried to get into the new construction market with some quality builders in our area and one guy told me, "Scott, we've got to hit a budget and people just don't care about the windows. They want a Jacuzzi tub, and they want the oak cabinets. When I sit down with them and explain that they can get a really good window for X amount or they can put the tub in, they'll choose the tub just about every time."

We talked a little about warranties. On a stock window, these typically don't cover as much as a custom-built window warranty will, and they're almost always for a shorter period of time. That said, you've also got to watch out for the people who are in business today, touting all these great warranties and products, but are out of business in five years. If you have a warranty in hand, but nobody is around to fulfill the obligations it outlines, it's a useless piece of paper. Again, the consumer gets stuck with whatever goes wrong when dealing with these fly-by-night companies.

Lastly, when shopping for stock windows, you're not likely to find nearly the selection of styles and features you can choose from when ordering custom windows. Why settle for less when you can have exactly what you want, made to order?

As with so many things in life, what looks like a bargain today can turn into a money pit tomorrow. Taken all together, a prudent homeowner will look beyond the immediate costs, to the significant savings realized over the long term when the job is done right.

KEEP IN MIND:

- Stock windows may look good, but may not fit properly without a significant amount of carpentry to your home.

- If you get stuck with a window that doesn't work properly after it's installed by a contractor, you can expect to get the runaround, because the contractor will say the window's defective, and the manufacturer will blame the installer.

- Be careful whom you work with; a guarantee from a contractor who goes out of business is a worthless piece of paper.

CHAPTER FIVE

HOW IMPORTANT IS INSTALLATION?

How important is the quality of installation and the company you choose to perform it, when it comes to your home? Here's an illustrative and by no means unique example. A couple of years ago, a fellow who used to work for us as an installer went out on his own and started a company installing windows. Recently, I heard that he went out of business and had left the state. This is a sad, familiar pattern with start-ups: the new owner gets in over his head and discovers he doesn't know how to run a business. Finally, he just gets sick of it, closes up shop, and moves to a different state so he doesn't have to worry about the aftermath of complaints from all the unhappy customers he's left behind. If something goes wrong for those folks and they need service, they're not going to get it from him.

What do you do in that case? Most likely, if it's a window issue you'll have another window company that will come out, which may or may not be familiar with the window that's been installed. They might not even know what brand it is, because a lot of manufacturers don't put their brand name on the window itself. If it's a problem with a manufacturer's defect, that manufacturer is probably not going to let somebody else do the work but will want the homeowners themselves to contact their customer service department, which will then ship the piece or part to the homeowner, for a fee, assuming the company is valid.

When that part or piece arrives, the new contractor or handyman will charge for the labor of the repair. Most installers will charge a service call fee of between $50 and $100 just to come out and look at it. Having diagnosed the problem and ordered the part, they'll have to make another trip out to install it, and that won't be free either.

When we do that kind of job for a customer who didn't install our window initially, we're able to quote them a fixed fee, because we know windows and we know how long the job will take. The last thing people want is to be quoted a price that goes up because the installer discovers the job will take longer than anticipated.

When it comes to installation, the knowledge and experience of the installer largely dictates whether the window will have future problems. It's generally best to work with a specialist rather than with a generalist, because a seasoned expert has run into most of the common and uncommon challenges that can come up and will know how to address them. For instance, our company only installs windows and doors. Our installers aren't doing windows one day, siding the next, and a frame job the following day. Why? Because our experience shows us that the jack-of-all-trades model doesn't work.

My father started his business with roofing. We did siding, windows, roofing, gutters, and downspouts and tried to juggle the window installation business in with the rest of the trades. But we have discovered that we can't let a roofing guy put siding on. He just beats everything up. Roofing is not as technical, and doesn't require the same degree of finesse that siding does. A roofer isn't required to be as careful or conscientious.

Windows aren't "forgiving" in terms of the ease of installation: Windows have to be put in square. They have to be properly installed in order to be operational, and they have to be insulated properly or your client will have airflow problems, air infiltration, and other potential issues. It requires a high degree of skill and a low tolerance for error. Our people are familiar with the kind of windows we build, which adds to customer's trust that we'll install them correctly, because every window is installed a little bit differently, according to the manufacturer's specifications.

If you find a window company that also does siding and roofing, make sure that there's a crew that specializes in window installation.

The same holds true in working with subcontractors: When you subcontract something out, you don't know what kind of work those guys did yesterday. They might have been building a house yesterday and are putting windows in today. You never really get specialized labor when you hire a subcontractor. If I, as a businessman, were to hire a subcontractor to work for me, I would have to send him to a window-installation training program of some sort in order for me to feel comfortable having him put our windows in. Typically, a freelance subcontractor is not going to do that because he wants to get in, get the installation done, get out, get paid, and go on to the next job. He is not an employee so he isn't really accountable.

A general contractor will often use subcontractors for different parts of a project to reduce costs. But if you need to repair or service any part of the improvement down the line, you might find that no one wants to take responsibility for it. The general contractor might tell you to talk to the subcontractor because the general contractor doesn't cover work done by a subcontractor, and the subcontractor might not cover anything at all. Even if you were guaranteed a lifetime warranty, any work done by a subcontractor might only be covered for a couple years, if it's even covered at all.

When you choose to hire a home improvement company that doesn't subcontract, you're getting a company with the in-house expertise to handle your project from start to finish, and you're getting dedication to undivided responsibility when it comes to service down the line. With a company that doesn't use subcontractors, there is no one to pass the buck to, so you know exactly who to go to for service if and when you need it.

A long time ago, we made a commitment to never use subcontractors for any of our work at AHT Wisconsin Windows. From measuring your window frames to get the right fit to the installation, and for 50 years after the job is done, we are the only contractors you'll have to deal with. We'll never shove the responsibility onto anyone else.

At the preinstallation point, accurate measurement taking is key. Obviously, if the window installers don't measure accurately, when your windows arrive, they're not going to fit. That does happen to us occasionally, because we're not perfect. Every now and then our production coordinator will make a mistake and we'll order a window that doesn't fit. Rather than try to modify the window to make it fit, we order a new one. That's not true of all companies; if they measure incorrectly and the window they get doesn't fit, they'll try to cobble it together somehow to make it fit. Ordering another window is always the most expensive way to do a job, and you don't make money when you do that. That's why we're careful, so that we know exactly what we need and it fits when we get it to the jobsite.

HOW DOES THE INSTALLATION PROCESS PROCEED?

Typically, it begins when the homeowner calls to set up an initial appointment. Our sales consultant will go to the home, and inspect the windows. He or she will sit down with the homeowner and go over the costs as well as the pros and cons of the different types of windows, along the lines of what we've covered in this book so far. Then, when the homeowner has weighed the options and made the choices, the sales consultant will fill out the paperwork along with a specification sheet, detailing exactly what the homeowner wants, so we're all clear about what was agreed upon.

We send a project coordinator to the home to get a list of materials needed and double check the measurements the sales consultant took to order the window. We have a specification sheet that specifies the color, measurements, and the styles, all the information pertaining to the window project. Our project coordinator will fill out the specification sheet, go through all the particulars with the homeowner, and check to see if there's any rotten wood that we're going to need to replace when we get there. Effectively, it's a bill of materials that we're going to require to get that project done, so we're not running around trying to find lumber and the various other things we need at the point of actual installation.

Typically, we receive the windows in about two weeks. Once we get them, we'll schedule the installation. We show up on the day and at the time we promised (which really should be the case with anyone you're working with), unless of course, it is raining cats and dogs or we are in the middle of a blizzard.

Typically, it only takes a day to install up to 8 to 10 windows, depending upon the difficulty. Not all installations are created equal, of course, but the rule of thumb is 8 to 10 windows.

Once the installation is complete and the homeowner has signed off on the paperwork, we do a walk-through to show the customer how to tilt the windows for easy cleaning, and to answer any questions. After the homeowner has completed the paperwork and payment, we send a little packet of materials with the warranty in it, instructions on how to clean the windows, and information on window condensation causes and cures, along with contact information.

IS IT OKAY TO WATCH?

Some homeowners are curious about how a window installation is done, and like to watch over the installer's shoulder. That's certainly within the homeowner's rights, and our installers are fine with that because they know what they're doing. Sometimes people actually pull up a chair, sit down and watch. Others prefer to wait until it's all done before taking their first look.

WHO SIGNS OFF ON THE INSTALLATION
WHEN THE JOB IS DONE?

Quality control is very important, and whoever installs your windows needs to have some system in place to check, after the job has been completed, to assure that you're happy with what has been done. When we finish an installation, we bring in a third party surveying company to make sure people are satisfied with the work. What we want from them is an unbiased report on how we did our job while we're there. The company that does the third-party surveys of our customers, Guild Quality, contacts the homeowners and keeps track of their opinions on our work. We're very proud to have received the Guild Quality With Distinction Award, which means that our company received a 90 percent plus positive rating, reflecting the percentage of customers who would refer our company to a friend. The use of a third-party survey makes sure we get honest and unbiased opinions. We use these surveys to keep our standards in line. In the rare instance that something bad does show up, we can take steps to correct it immediately

WHEN IS THE OPTIMAL TIME FOR YOU
TO INSTALL NEW WINDOWS?

Most folks assume that once it starts snowing in November, and until the snow is melted in March or April, you can't install windows if it's cold out. That's not the case, because we do window installations all year long. The fact is that there is no bad time to install windows.

Some homeowners don't want us opening up their house when it's five degrees outside because they're worried about the loss of heat. However, with a replacement window that's measured exactly to the opening, once we get the old window out, it's probably less than 10 minutes before the new window is installed. Within 10 minutes the window is going to be in and, while it won't be completely sealed and done, it'll be in to the point where there isn't a lot of cold air coming in. The little bit of heat that is lost by doing the installation in the winter will be gained back within a week or even less, thanks to the new window's higher energy efficiency. The same thing goes for installation in the summer, although, then, people are not ordinarily as concerned about letting heat in briefly. The other benefit to a winter installation is that you can feel the difference the windows make right after they are installed. We often hear, "We can feel the difference already."

INSULATION

For years, most installers used fiberglass in insulating windows, but now we use nonexpanding foam. Unlike some other foam products, it expands to the point where it seals up but it doesn't overexpand and push everything out of alignment. This helps with air infiltration because even with fiberglass insulation, if the wind is blowing, there's a certain amount that gets through the insulation. The bottom line is that you want to make sure that it's an insulation that's water repellant and sealed and prevents air infiltration.

LEAD PAINT

Another issue, particularly with older homes, is the presence of lead paint. The EPA came out with rules and regulations on how to deal with lead paint if you come in contact with it. Whether you're a siding contractor or do windows or roofing, if the home you're working on has lead paint on it, you have to take certain precautions. There are not a lot of people who are dependably doing so. Certainly the fly-by-night window guys are not addressing the issue. It's something that we're very conscientious about. All our installation employees are trained on how to handle lead paint. There is a very specific set of protocols to be followed, and they need to be followed to the letter.

Of course, it costs a little more money to do a lead paint job but, at the same time, we're conscious of the safety factor, both for the homeowner and for ourselves. It's not an area in which you can or should skimp. If the house was built before 1978, whether there's lead in it or not, we have to treat it as if there were.

CLEANUP

Cleanup should never be an issue for the homeowner, but it can be if your contractor or his crew isn't careful. Make sure that when you're checking out a window installer, you ask about his guarantee on leaving the areas he's working on exactly as he found them.

We want to make sure that the job is cleaned up when we're done. I don't want any reports of our guys leaving any job-related debris. All the windows that we take out of the house, and anything that's related to the installation, we take with us and we properly dispose of it. Homeowners are never left with a mess to clean up on their own. If we're taking out a door or something from a home, and the homeowners have a cabin they want to use it on and they ask us to leave it behind, then we'll leave it there. If they don't want it, we'll take it and dispose of it. That doesn't always happen with other contractors, especially with subcontractors.

FOLLOW-UP

Not typically, but every now and then, customers find that what they thought they were getting is different than what they got. In those cases, we go out to the homeowners and we discuss what might have gone wrong, and what needs to be done to make it right.

It's important to know, as a homeowner, that there are a lot of people who won't go back and do that kind of service. The reason they don't is because they're too busy installing the next job or doing paperwork after the job, and they just don't have time to make that follow-up call. They've got to make a dollar and they probably didn't charge enough for it to start with, so they're out trying to make a living and now they've got to go back and service. It's just never something they want to do. Some of them may actually want to do it but can't because of time restraints, and they can't afford to hire someone to do it for them.

Then there are some people who just pass through, like storm chasers. For instance, in our area, when you have a hailstorm, this kind of operator comes through here, takes on a lot of low-cost contracts, does the jobs with shoddy workmanship, and blows out of town. Now the homeowners are stuck with that result, which sometimes is more bad than good.

There are certain things that you have to charge for in order to stay in business. Sometimes it costs a little more one year or a little less one year than it did the year before or year after, but if you don't have somebody on staff who's dedicated to doing service, it just won't get done.

Here's the other catch-22: If I came to your home to give you an estimate and laid out our service guarantees, and another contractor gives you an estimate that is less money, and that contractor promises you the same things (even though he may not actually have a dedicated service guy), you're going to question the discrepancy in price. Likely, you'll say, "Well, I had another guy here who gave me a lower price, and who talked about service too. He told me that if there's anything that goes wrong, he'll come back and take care of it." Unfortunately, what you're told isn't always what's going to happen when someone's trying to convince you to sign a contract. Your only hope is to call some of that contractor's previous customers and ask about their experiences. Even the storm chasers will promise service, though, in fact, they'll be in a different state when a problem happens. They tell you whatever you want to hear sometimes. A good rule of thumb is that if they've been in business in the area for years and years, it's likely that they've got a good record of customer service and satisfaction. You can't stay in business in a small town like Clintonville, which has a population of about 4,500 people, if you don't do a good job. And we have hundreds of small towns in Wisconsin we work in each year.

The other thing you can do is to check the company out with the Better Business Bureau (BBB). Although it's really not a government agency of any kind and won't go to a company on your behalf and say, "You have to fix this thing for this particular person," the bureau does have an arbitration program, and a company that's listed with it has to agree to use arbitration if there's a dispute.

This is how it works: Let's say I did business for you and we put everything in exactly the way it was supposed to be, but you say, "I'm not satisfied, because I paid $12,000 for these windows and I only got $10,000 worth of value." In that situation, an arbitrator will come from the Better Business Bureau and sit between us. He'll listen to my story and then he'll listen to your story and then he'll make a decision on who's going to do what. Whatever decision the arbitrator makes, both you and I have to agree ahead of time that this decision is final. It's not a service that we've ever had to use, fortunately, but we do talk about it when we meet with the client, initially, in the home, because people don't want to be taken advantage of.

When a company is a member of the Better Business Bureau and has an A+ rating, that business will take care of its customers, because people don't hesitate to pick up the phone and call the Better Business Bureau to report a business they're unhappy with. There are companies in our area that have a D rating or a C rating with the Better Business Bureau. Companies that don't take care of their customers are the ones with those low ratings. We're proud of our A+ rating. It says something about how we take care of our customers.

THE BOTTOM LINE

Know whom you're dealing with before you sign a contract. Do your due diligence: check their references, their standing with the BBB, and remember, if a deal looks too good to be true, it almost certainly is. You don't want to wind up with a houseful of problems and nothing but what I call a "taillight warranty," which is one that runs out when your contractor finishes the project and pulls out of your driveway. When you can't see his taillights anymore, your warranty's gone too.

KEEP IN MIND:

- When looking for a window installer, go with a specialist, not a generalist.

- Ask your contractor if he/she will be subcontracting your job. If so, who's responsible if there's a problem? (Get it in writing.)

- A low price should not necessarily be your main consideration when investing in windows for your home.

- Remember: The bitterness of poor quality is long remembered after the sweetness of low price is forgotten.

- Ask for references—and check them!

CHAPTER SIX

PRICE AND LONG-TERM VALUE

What kind of replacement windows and installation will meet your needs? Start by looking at the style you've got now. Do you like it, or are you ready for a change? If you've got double-hung windows, you can swap them for casement styles. If you've got a big picture window, a bay window might be an attractive substitute, one that protrudes from the house and gives you room inside for a cozy window seat. Those are some of the options that you can consider.

If, like most of us, you're concerned with reducing heating and cooling costs, once you put a replacement window in, whatever heat or cooling costs you save go into your pocket. It's a continued saving that you'll reap through the years and certainly deserves to be figured into the cost-versus-benefit equation.

READ THE WARRANTY

One of the things to consider as you weigh the price of new windows is the warranty on a window and how long that warranty's going to last, because that's going to determine how far into the future your energy savings can be figured against your cost for the window. In other words, if your window has a 10-year warranty and, after 10 years, you have to buy another window because something's gone wrong with the one you installed, now you're out more money and your costs will outrun your savings. If you put a high-quality window in that has a good warranty of, say, 50 years, even if it's more expensive at the outset, it will save you money and bother in the long run. Well-made modern windows will pay for themselves in energy savings alone, especially in climates as extreme as Wisconsin's.

Added to that is the convenience of having windows that work properly and are, typically, easier to clean than old-fashioned ones, in addition to being more durable. The ability to clean your tilt-in windows from inside the home is a great advantage.

SAFETY AND SECURITY

Home security and safety are issues that people often overlook when considering window replacement, but they're certainly worth adding into the equation. Are the locks on your windows functional, or just decorative? By that I mean that if a lock is of poor quality and not secured to the window properly, it's all too easy for a thief to take a pry bar, pop your window open and come into your home. You want to make sure that the locks are sturdy enough to prevent that from happening.

SEEING YOUR HOME AS OTHERS SEE IT

In talking about home values, you hear a lot about "curb appeal," and high-quality replacement windows can add a lot of curb appeal in terms of your home's overall appearance. If you replace a flat picture window with a decorative bay, and a plain entry door with a nicer one that has leaded glass, it adds to your home's personality and attractiveness. That's enough to get a home shopper to request a showing, and that can lead to a quicker sale at a higher price. People don't always notice the specifics when they're home shopping, but when they see a home with well-maintained, high-quality windows, they notice that, for some reason, the house looks better than another place down the street. And those who do notice your windows will draw a positive conclusion about your overall standard of home maintenance, which also adds value in the buyer's eyes. Conversely, peeling or obviously worn-out windows may make the potential buyer wonder what else you may have let slide, and that's not a good thing.

THINK GREEN

Most informed people today are adherents of the idea of "going green." We don't want to see our landfills overflowing with unwanted building materials that won't biodegrade. When you buy a quality window—one that has a 50-year warranty—you're helping prevent that from happening. True, a window's frames still take petroleum products to make, but the fact that the window is built to last means that, over that long term, it's a "green" window, because when you compare it to the life span of a 10-year window, you won't have to replace it five times.

PRICE AND COST ARE NOT ALWAYS THE SAME THING

In our experience, as far as costs are concerned, we see three different types of consumers. The first type is the cost-obsessed consumer whose only consideration is the immediate expense involved. If the window you're showing him or her isn't the cheapest one on the market, she or he won't buy it. Some people just live their lives like that. The cheapest one is the one they're going to buy and they'll buy it every 5 or 10 years and still think they're going to save money. If you offer them a window that's going to last five times as long as the cheapest one they're considering, they'll still go for the cheaper option, somehow figuring that they'll save money on the deal even if they have to replace the windows five times. It's not logical, but there it is.

Then you have the do-it-yourselfer. These are the folks who are going to buy a lumberyard window because the cost is $100 or $150 or whatever, and they'll put it in themselves. Like cost-obsessed consumers, they buy low-end materials no matter what, and there's no way you can logically talk them out of it.

Finally, you have people who will buy a quality window if you show it to them and explain the benefits. The primary aim of this book is to help educate and inform that thoughtful consumer on what to look for, what to pay for, and what not to pay for, when buying a window.

There are companies out there that take that same $150 lumberyard, low-end window and charge the consumer $1,500 for it. Now, you've added insult to injury. You've got a low-quality, junk window, but you're paying a premium for it. Unfortunately, that kind of tactic is more common in the window industry than we'd like it to be, which is why being an informed consumer is so vital. Those who are preyed upon in this way by unscrupulous companies go into the deal only knowing what the salesperson told them. What our company does is educate people on the possibilities available to them in windows and let them make an informed decision on what they want to buy. Of course, we want it to be our product, but at the same time we want to give value. When they spend $10,000 on windows, we want them to know they got $10,000+ in value.

Another piece of the price equation is the guarantee of service down the line. We've talked about how consumers are sometimes trapped between their installer/sales person and the manufacturer when something goes wrong after the window is in. Nobody likes to get the runaround, and in those cases, the consumer is too often the loser. Part of an honest company's price is the guarantee that you'll never have to face a situation like that and that if and when you need it, service will be there for you without question. Our product pricing includes the security of knowing that we're there when our customers need us to provide the service they require. Down the line, in the years to come, we're still going to be there, because we didn't price the installation so cheaply that we can't stay in business and be there for our customers.

There are so many hidden costs lurking when you choose the cheap route, things that may not be immediately evident as you're making your choice but can come back to bite you down the line. That window you carry out of the home store may have a low price tag on it, but chances are that you're going to pay a lot more in the long run. There are so many things that can go wrong with that approach. Number one, now that you've purchased the window, you've got to find somebody to install it, so you call a local handyman. He'll tell you he knows what he's doing, but does he really know how to install *your* window? Anybody in the construction industry or home improvement can install a window and they've probably installed hundreds of windows, but was it that particular brand, that type, with its specific type of installation? They're all a little different. Just because someone has installed one brand of window doesn't mean he or she can do yours properly. The fact is an installer has to be stellar at what he or she does to make the thing operate properly. If it doesn't, you're most likely going to be left holding the bag—and out shopping for another new window.

THE "BARGAIN" THAT WASN'T

It's been said that "the bitterness of poor quality is long remembered after the sweetness of low price is forgotten," and that's very true of shoddy work done on your home, which is probably your biggest investment. The English writer and critic John Ruskin said:

"It's unwise to pay too much, but it's worse to pay too little. When you pay too much, you lose a little money. That is all. When you pay too little, you sometimes lose everything because the thing you bought was incapable of doing the thing it was bought to do. The common law of business balance prohibits paying a little and getting a lot. It can't be done. If you deal with the lowest bidder, it is well to add something for the risk you run and if you do that, you'll have enough to pay for something better."

Everybody has a nightmare story about the "bargain" that turns out not to be. How many times have we bought a middle-of-the-road choice to save money and then ended up regretting it when we discovered it just wasn't satisfactory? I know I have. Usually, the thing in question was still too expensive to allow us to justify just tossing it and purchasing the more expensive version we should have bought in the first place. So now we're stuck with our unsatisfactory choice for keeps.

It's the same with windows. Folks will choose between a cheaper company and us; if our bid was $15,000, they go ahead and put the cheaper outfit's $10,000 worth of windows in their home. If those window don't perform as promised, they're not going to tear them out of their house and put $15,000 worth back in. Rather than that, they'll live with that bad choice for about 10 years until the product is falling apart and they get sufficiently fed up and say, "We should have just done it. Let's get it done right."

In that 10 years, you lose a lot of money in fuel costs thanks to lower energy efficiency, and you're likely to have a lot of frustration thanks to issues with shoddy construction, such as balance systems that don't work. All of that adds up to more than the additional costs you'd have incurred making the more prudent choice in the first place. You can avoid all these window woes by going with the best, because the best won't fail you and will be there for you if and when you need service.

Here in Wisconsin energy efficiency is really number one on the list when people go window shopping. They want energy efficiency and they want ease of cleaning, and they want no maintenance. Those are the top three considerations on their lists, over and over again. Esthetic appeal and the desire to make an upgrade or update the appearance of the home are other considerations, but the first three are by far the ones our clients most frequently cite. Spending more at the outset may seem like unnecessary expense, but remember, it includes the true value of the warranty, and the added energy efficiency, because that's what's going to pay for the window. In addition to energy efficiency, it's going to increase the resale value of the home. When you go to sell your home in the future, the quality you pay for today will be reflected in the price you realize on the sale, so you're going to get a return on the investment there also. The cause and effect of cost versus value across the country is reported regularly by such media as the *Wall Street Journal* and *Remodeling Contractor* magazine. If you install, say, new kitchen cabinets, or a new bath, windows, siding, or roofing, what is going to be the return on your investment? Most people recoup about 75 percent of the window cost. If they were to put the windows in today and sell the house tomorrow, they would get about 75 percent of their investment back. That's a high percentage before even beginning to factor in fuel savings. Added to that is the fact that, of course, you don't have to maintain the windows anymore. You don't have to scrape them, paint them, putty them, or keep putting on storm windows and taking them off again. You may shrug that off if you're a do-it-yourselfer, figuring you can just do that work yourself, but really, what would you rather be doing with your time? Scraping windows, or golfing, spending time with your kids, or doing whatever you'd be doing if you didn't have that chore? Your time is worth quite a bit when you come to think of it, and I'm guessing that scraping and painting your windows isn't at the top of your list when it comes to things you want to spend your time doing.

KEEP IN MIND:

- Top-quality windows add significant resale value to your home.

- Make sure that your contractor spells out exactly what his contract covers.

- Just because someone has installed windows before doesn't mean they're qualified to install YOUR windows.

CHAPTER SEVEN

CHOOSING THE RIGHT CONTRACTOR

W hat should you be considering as you choose a contractor? One of the big things to look for is somebody that
has the proper insurance. Be aware that there are a lot of
contractors out there that don't carry liability insurance, which covers
the costs of anything they accidentally damage in your home. And
accidents do happen; every now and then a ladder could slip and go
through the window. Usually, homeowners have liability insurance,
although not all of them do. But what happens in a case like that
is that if you, as the homeowner, have contracted with someone to
come into your home and do a project for you, typically, the liability
insurance on your homeowner's policy doesn't cover that worker,
because you're paying him to do it. It might cover somebody who
comes and helps you on a weekend. There are a lot of people out
there whose friends come over to help them roof the house, for
instance, but these friends are not paid to help with the work. In that
case, the policy may cover you, but that protection doesn't necessarily
extend to the situation in which you've hired labor. In those cases, the

contractor needs to have a separate liability insurance policy to make sure you're covered.

Accidents do happen, and you don't want to be left asking who's going to cover those expenses. If the contractor doesn't have liability insurance, then you're stuck as a homeowner if damage is done to your home or if someone is injured on your property. It's a nightmare scenario, but in today's litigious society, all too possible.

Then, in addition to liability insurance, the people working for your contractor have to be covered by workers' compensation. Whether your contractor is insuring his workers to the extent that the law requires here in Wisconsin can become an issue for you as the homeowner in the event that one of those workers is injured on the job. If you've got people working on your house who don't have workers' compensation insurance, and someone falls off a ladder and winds up with a lot of medical bills, that could be put on you, the homeowner, because the other guy doesn't have insurance. When people get hurt, they look for whoever can pay for it.

In our case, if one of our workers were to fall off a ladder, our workers' compensation takes care of him, pays the medical bills, pays him for not being able to work—all those costs are covered. Not all contractors are similarly conscientious in this area, and it's something that can potentially create big problems for you as the homeowner. Why have that hanging over your head when you're hiring somebody to do a job for you? The risk should be theirs, not yours. You should certainly make sure that anyone you're considering as a contractor does have, at the very least, liability and workers' compensation policies.

If you're hiring an individual rather than a company to do your installation for you, that person doesn't need to have workers' compensation insurance but should have liability coverage in addition to some kind of disability insurance in the event that he is injured while on the job.

Another consideration we've discussed a little before is whether or not the person or company you're considering is a specialty contractor, and by that I mean a company whose business is concentrated on the kind of work that you need done rather than on work of a more general scope. It makes sense to use a company that specializes, in the same way that you'd certainly choose a heart surgeon over a general practitioner if you needed heart surgery. Why? Because that professional is expert in his or her field with experience that's vital to your well-being.

That speaks to the concern that many people have about cost as well. If you were to experience a heart attack and you needed a heart surgeon, would you run around, trying to figure out which surgeon was the cheapest or would you choose somebody who specialized in heart surgery, someone you know is going to do the best job possible to save your life? People don't typically go hunting for a low-ball estimate like that when their health is at stake, nor should they. When you're talking about your home, in most cases that's your single biggest investment, which should be a powerful incentive to put quality ahead of price.

When interviewing prospective contractors, an important thing to know is how long they've been in business. They should be more than willing to provide references and contact information, so that you can check on their previous customers' satisfaction with the jobs they did. Do they have a customer list that they're willing to share with you? Some people don't or won't. Be wary if they refuse, or don't want you to call people for whom they've worked in the past. Part of being a smart consumer and protecting yourself from less than reliable contractors is the willingness to do the due diligence. Don't simply take their word for it.

Even I, who should know better, occasionally do the dumb thing and get called out by not doing my own due diligence. Recently a neighbor of mine was having some painting done and using a local guy to do it. I had an ugly shed at the back of my house that needed a coat of paint, so I hired this painter without asking around about his reputation before I did so. I figured since the neighbors had hired him, he must be okay. He wasn't, as it turned out. Not only was the paint job second rate, but he took forever to finish it. He did an okay job in the end, but I really had to prod him just to get it done.

When you're shopping for a contractor, it's also a good idea to ask about terms of payment. If anybody wants 100 percent of the payment up front, I would certainly shy away from them. There's no reason for that kind of thing ever, in my opinion. That being said, every now and then, when we work with customers who use a finance company to pay for their windows, they'll occasionally pay us 100 percent ahead of time. More typically, because we install custom-ordered products and no financing is involved and the customers write us a check upon completion, we ask for 50 percent down and the other 50 percent when the job is completed and the customers are satisfied. Your satisfaction at the end of the day is the big thing you want to have guaranteed, and it should be a requirement for whichever contractor you're working with. We don't expect people to pay unless they're satisfied. If they're not satisfied, we didn't do our job in one way, shape, or form, and that needs to be ironed out, figured out, and done before we ask for payment. Again, stay away from anyone who wants 100 percent down. If you're looking at custom windows, a 50 percent down payment should be acceptable and the final payment should be contingent upon your satisfaction.

If you're going down to the lumberyard to buy a stock window, you should be able to get the thing installed for you without a down payment, and you should be very wary of anyone who asks for a down payment under those circumstances. There are so many people who will take half down on a home improvement project and never show up again to do the work. They're just gone, and good luck tracking them down. Shady operators like that give the whole home improvement industry a black eye. We occasionally hear these stories from customers who've been burned by an unreliable contractor in the past, so they're understandably nervous about giving us the initial down payment. Fortunately, since we've been in business since 1967, we've got thousands of people that new customers can call to find out what kind of a job we do. That usually puts them at ease.

I certainly hear of situations in which customers aren't willing to sign off on their completion paperwork and usually it's because of something that the contractor didn't properly explain at the beginning of the project. The reason they're not satisfied is the person who sold them the product didn't properly set up the expectations ahead of time. Maybe the salesperson didn't show them an actual window but sold them a window described in a brochure. Perhaps the salesperson didn't explain in detail and put into their agreement exactly what was going to be done.

Then the workmen show up at the site with the windows and the homeowner says, "Wait a minute. I didn't order this window." This is poor practice on the contractor's part because the job is already in the red at the start. Sometimes at that point the contractor makes an offer, along the lines of, "Well, I'll give you a discount if you take them anyway."

In my experience, giving customers a discount to satisfy them never actually satisfies them, because they don't get what they want. That means that every time they bring their friends or relatives to their home, they say, "Well, I didn't get what I wanted, but he gave me a discount." That's not a happy customer, and that's not how you build a good reputation. If people say to me, "I'm going to be completely satisfied. Give me $1,000 off and I'll keep the product as-is," I'll talk to them personally and say, "Are you sure? I know that doesn't usually satisfy somebody and I'd rather just reorder the window or do whatever I've got to do to fix it rather than give you a discount." As a consumer myself, I have had contractors offer to discount the price of work they didn't do properly, and I've gone along with it, but never without subsequently regretting that choice and wishing that I'd insisted on getting what I originally wanted and expected.

Bottom line: *don't accept a contractor's word that he'll be there for you and will do a good job without demanding references and taking the time to check those references yourself.* Look for someone who's been in business long enough to build a good reputation, because he's more likely to be there down the line if and when you have a problem with the work or materials. Don't just look at price, because it's not a good predictor of quality, and the money you save today won't seem like a bargain if the windows you've paid for let you down.

KEEP IN MIND:

- When interviewing a contractor, find out how long he or she has been in business.

- Make sure your contractor has sufficient workers' compensation and liability insurance to cover your home and you in case of an accident, because most often your homeowner's policy does not extend to cover workers you pay to do work on your home or accidental damage they may cause to your property.

- Never get talked into paying 100 percent down on a window replacement job (or any home improvement). A reputable contractor will never ask for more than 50 percent, and an installer shouldn't ask for a down payment at all.

CHAPTER EIGHT

CHOOSING A FRONT DOOR

W e've talked a lot about windows and the impact they have on your home's energy efficiency, appearance, and security, and hopefully you're now a better-informed consumer than you were when you started reading this book. Let's talk a little about a related topic: your front door.

Considering how long you've had your current entry door, it's easy to see why you keep it. It's served you well and been reliable for years. It opens and shuts without a problem, although it may squeak on occasion. But over the course of time, it may not be meeting all of your needs anymore. Those needs include maintaining energy efficiency and providing adequate home security.

The first impression your home makes depends greatly on the look of your front door. Most of us have lived with our front doors so long that we hardly notice them, unless of course they're no longer functioning right. But the look of your door can add a lot—or detract a lot—from the overall appearance of your home, and deserves more than a cursory glance. Take a moment to "see yourself as others see you" when they look at your home. What does your front door say about you?

When someone looks at the front of a house and sees a nice leaded glass door, it makes a positive impression. We call it curb appeal in our business, and it's a big piece of what drives your home's eventual resale value. Generally, people who are house hunting will initially check out all the homes that are for sale in their price range by driving by them.

When they drive by and see one that has curb appeal, they might not know what it is about the house that's appealing, but there's something about it that makes it look like "home." It could be the fact that there's no peeling paint around the windows and the frames. It could be because there's a handsome, leaded-glass door versus an ordinary door. The lookers can't always put their finger on it, but they know they want to get inside.

Conversely, a home with a beaten-up-looking door, one with peeling paint or sagging on its hinges, is likely to turn that buyer off. It says that the owner may not care as much about his house's condition as he should, and that there may well be other issues related to maintenance that are less visible but that have also been neglected. That's not the impression you want to make, unless you're looking for a DIY-type buyer in the market for a fixer-upper at a lowball price. You could just accept it or decide it's time to make a change. For the sake of this discussion, let's say you decide to make the change and switch to a new door. But where do you begin?

Looking for a new long-term relationship with your entry door should begin carefully. The quality of the door and reputation of the manufacturer are important. It's also helpful to consider who will be handling the installation. There are a handful of different things you'll want to consider before purchasing a replacement door, so here are some ideas to get you started on the right path.

Doors do wear out, and a surprising number of people will put up with a faulty door or they'll use a different entryway if the front door is sticking. But problems with the door's obvious functions aren't necessarily the only ones you can have with a worn-out door. As long as it opens and shuts and the locking mechanisms work, you don't really think about other problems, such as how much air infiltration there could be because of worn-out or nonexistent weather stripping. Sometimes it's actually visible, but most people don't put their recliners in front of the door, so they don't feel the air come in. They certainly don't think about conduction, which we've discussed in terms of windows but which can also be an issue with a door.

Security is certainly another important issue. There are a lot of old doors that just have a doorknob, not a deadbolt. It's fairly easy to break into a home via a doorknob that has no additional locking mechanism, most of the time simply using a credit card. When there's a deadbolt, you can't get in unless you actually break the door down and wreck the frame. With just a doorknob, it's not a secure door. There are certain knobs that are better in that regard than others, but if it's got just a doorknob and no deadbolt, there's a way in.

Older doors are also often a significant point of energy loss, in heat or cooling. Sometimes older doors don't have weather stripping on them at all, especially the older wooden doors. You can always try to add weather stripping of course, but honestly, it never looks right, and it almost always leaves leakage. Newer doors do come with better weather stripping and are more energy efficient.

Also, the door itself is often not energy efficient due to its composition. Doors on older homes are frequently made of wood, and wood is not an insulator. In contrast, modern steel doors are built with insulation in them. Some are better than others and have denser foam between the steel panels, so they're more energy efficient.

Let's talk a little about conduction as it applies to doors. You'll remember that conduction is basically the transfer of heat or cold through an object. If you have 90-degree heat beating on the door from outside, eventually it's going to be conducted inside through the door. It's just a matter of time. That's why we have to turn our furnaces on to heat our house up in winter. Half an hour later, the furnace has to kick in and heat up the house again, because that heat is being conducted outside, even through insulation. Well-insulated doors and windows slow down the rate of conduction, but heat still conducts through them at some rate or other. There's even a measurable rate of conduction through a wall, depending on whether the air is hotter or colder outside. When it comes to energy efficiency, it's all just a matter of slowing down the rate of heat conduction. It's our business to slow that rate down to the greatest extent possible.

Some people claim that they can eliminate heat conduction altogether, but it's impossible. Everything has a conduction rate. And it's worth noting that if your door has glass in it, and that door is more than five years old, it almost certainly is not energy efficient, so you're losing heat at that point too.

So, how do you know when it's time to replace your front door? The problems to look for are:

- Deteriorated weather stripping: You'll recognize the problem in winter if you can feel cold air coming in underneath your door or along the sides of it.

- It doesn't fit properly because it's sagged or warped over the years, so you may have difficulty closing or opening it.

- Your locking system no longer functions properly, or is inadequate (limited to a simple doorknob lock) for proper security.

- The door itself is rotting, chipping, peeling, or cracking. This is more likely to be a problem with the older wooden doors that most houses used to be fitted with.

- Rusting due to a steel door gone bad (probably only came with a primer coat and was not subsequently properly finished).

Okay, you've decided that it's time to do something about your worn-out front door. What are the options available to you, and how do they differ?

The bottom-of-the-line solution would be to simply replace the door itself by buying one without a frame at a home improvement store. Of course, there's no guarantee that the so-called standard size is actually going to fit in your home's doorframe properly, given that houses shift and sag to some extent over time. So hanging it may not, in fact, be as simple as you imagine, nor might the fit be right.

The next step up is a prehung door. Prehung means that it has hinges and a frame and it's already in that frame. It doesn't have a doorknob or locking mechanism installed, but typically it has the hole for the doorknob and deadbolt. It's primed but unpainted. If it has glass in it, it'll either be leaded glass or clear glass. The clear glass isn't triple pane; the leaded glass always is, in that the leaded glass is in between two sheets of clear glass, but it doesn't have the krypton gas that provides good insulation that you'll find in higher-quality products.

A prefinished door would be the next step up in terms of quality. This door is likely to be prehung as well, although the frame won't be finished because you have to paint it to match your house. Again, the doorknob and locking mechanism aren't provided, so you'd need to purchase those on top of the door itself.

Beyond the stock in a home improvement store, you'd be looking at a custom-built door. You order the color and the style and choose the kind of hinges and hardware you want. The company that sells you the door would also install it. Without a doubt, this is the most trouble-free and high-quality option.

People sometimes think that all you need to do is buy a door, because they assume doors are standard sizes, but that's not always the case. Years ago, manufacturers sometimes made doors 31 inches wide instead of 32. For some houses, you have to purchase a custom entry door because the standard door is not as high as it needs to be to fit the door frame, or it might be too wide. There are fewer things you can do to customize a door than to customize a window, but typically, it's the height that is the problem. Especially for the DIY guy, trying to retrofit one to an existing frame, the installation can be very frustrating, and the result unsatisfactory. I bought my first home in the early '80s when I was first married, and I tried to put a front door on that house. It was just a miserable experience (and I've been around the home improvement business most of my life!). They didn't have custom-built doors back then, so I assumed I could make it work. It's just another example of the kind of home improvement project that can look simple but turn into a real can of worms.

When you're door shopping, there are several options available in terms of materials. Wood, steel, and fiberglass are the primary options.

Not many wood doors are built any more, although there are some really high-end companies that make customized wooden doors for million-dollar-plus homes. These are strictly specialty items, and very pricey.

Fiberglass doors are gaining ground, despite having gotten a deservedly bad reputation in years past, largely because of problems that have subsequently been solved. If you want an aesthetically pleasing door that looks like wood, fiberglass is probably a nice option as far as a door is concerned. Years ago, they warped terribly. They wouldn't close against the weather stripping and so would let air in. I decided not to use them because of that, but it seems that certain manufacturers have resolved that issue now. Another issue with fiberglass doors was that the finish simply didn't wear as well as it should, again, because of the material's tendency to expand and contract in extreme weather. Even washing could rub the finish off it and the problem was particularly noticeable around the doorknob, where it got a lot of wear. I've seen that personally. I don't have any fiberglass doors in my own home, but friends of mine do and they don't look great after about five years of use. If you try to paint a fiberglass door, you've voided the warranty on the finish, and that paint probably won't wear well either, so you're effectively compounding the problem, not solving it. Based on what I've seen go wrong, in the past, with fiberglass doors, I prefer not to sell and install them.

The most popular, practical, and durable door made is a steel entry door. Typically, this is made up of two sheets of steel with the space between them filled with insulating foam. The density of that foam dictates how energy efficient the door slab itself is. Different gauges of steel are used. Twenty-six gauge is the most popular one, but unfortunately, it will dent and bend, particularly if someone kicks it, which can also be an issue as far as security is concerned. Let's say you have a deadbolt and when you deploy the deadbolt, it goes into the frame an inch and a quarter. If the door is a high-quality door, when somebody tries to kick it in and if the deadbolt doesn't give out, they're not going to get in. If you have a 26-gauge door, even if the deadbolt did its job, a determined burglar could kick the door enough to bend it to the point where the deadbolt won't hold. When we install a door we add a plate to the backside of the jamb, so when the deadbolt goes into the jamb, the metal protects the wood frame from breaking. The deadbolt is only as secure as the frame it is in.

The thicker the steel, the better quality the door, but when you go to a big box store you're not likely to find anything but the thinnest steel, because those doors are in the price point market rather than the quality market. Another important thing to know if you're looking at prefabricated, home-store-type steel doors is that they come primed but not painted, and if you don't paint them within a set period of time, you're voiding your warranty. Driving around, I see a lot of doors that have never had a top coat painted over that initial primer coat. Over the years they look dingier and dingier, and finally, they start rusting and looking horrible.

A steel door requires less maintenance than any other type. It's stable, it doesn't expand and contract like a fiberglass door, and it's more energy-efficient than a fiberglass door. That's why it's the most popular; it fits just about everybody's needs. It can be made up in nearly any style. It's also energy efficient. In Wisconsin especially, we have a conduction problem and around the edge of the door, if you don't have a weather break between the outside and the inside, you get condensation. If your house has higher concentrations of moisture, you're going to get either ice and/or condensation forming on the inside of your door. This problem is specific to areas like ours where typical winter temperatures plunge to zero or below. If your door isn't right for our climate, you'll have that problem.

When you are thinking about buying a brand new door, color is most likely one of the first things on your mind. Working with color on your front door is a great chance to draw attention to your home from the curb and make a memorable first impression. When choosing a color for your door, finding the right balance of contrast and continuity is key. You want to make the door "pop" without looking gaudy or out of place.

In general, if your home is a darker color, go with a lighter color door, and vice versa. Houses with muted/neutral tones can benefit from the boldness of a vibrantly colored door. If you have a brick home, consider a dark-green door, as it'll complement the red of the brick well.

Just like the color of the door itself, you will get the biggest impact with hardware through contrast. Try to pick hardware with finishing that will stand out from the door, and even better if it matches the rest of your house's trim at the same time. There are a wide variety of style options for hardware beyond the finish, from traditional to modern and in-between, so choose pieces that are going to fit the overall feel of your home.

Style is entirely a matter of personal preference. Some people have a door with two sidelights, one on either side. Some people opt for a door with a single sidelight, and others have none. Then it's a matter of choosing the color that would accent your home. You can even get a wood-grain finish in any number of colors. Recently, we toured the factory where our doors are made. I met with the lady who does the finish work on the doors we install, and it was just phenomenal to hear her talk about it and see the level of perfectionism she brings to her work. It can't go out with one blemish on it. It's got to be perfect.

Hardware style too is mostly a matter of personal preference. There are several finishes available: bright brass, antique brass, nickel, or bronze, which has an aged look. In choosing your hardware, quality counts—and beauty goes much more than skin deep. Too often folks go to the hardware section at their local Home Depot or Menard's and start looking at doorknobs. The most expensive at that kind of store will run about $150. People look at that price and say, "This one over here is kind of similar, but it's only $65. I'm going to buy this one." What they don't take into consideration is that the more expensive one isn't more expensive for no reason. It's usually better quality, which means both the finish and the locking mechanism will hold up longer and better than the good-looking cheap version will.

The kind of hardware we use isn't sold in big box stores, because it's higher quality and bargain hunters won't buy it. Typically, it has a better quality finish, and a better warranty, and because this is something you're going to want to keep for many years, that warranty really matters. Another thing to consider is service, in case anything does go wrong. We've been installing doors for a long time. We might put a door in and 10 years later get a call saying that the thumb latch isn't working, so we go out and see what's wrong. After 10 years, Home Depot is not going to come out to your house to fix your lock, and if you take it out of your door and back to the store, the store won't do anything about it. It's just not designed to operate that way.

Glass in a door is an attractive option; it lets more light into your home, and is decorative from the outside. Some people prefer not to have it at eye level, because of the privacy factor, and typically, mounting some sort of a shade on a door isn't feasible. Leaded glass can solve the privacy problem, and is also especially decorative.

If you go with glass whether clear or leaded, you've got multiple style options to consider: full lights, half rounds, and many others. In the leaded-glass category, you'll have additional options in the look of the glass you select.

And you don't have to sacrifice energy efficiency if you go with a top-quality door. Again, that's not going to be a door you can find at your local lumberyard. It doesn't make sense to buy a high-quality door that's energy efficient and then blow it by using the standard double-pane glass. There go your savings, in terms of higher fuel bills.

As with windows, many of the problems homeowners face when they buy a door are connected to improper installation. Even for a dedicated weekend warrior, installing something as big as a door can be so daunting that you'll realize it's beyond your skill set. Typically, you go to a big box store to buy a door, but you don't have anybody to install it. You ask the guy who sells you the door for a recommendation, and he'll show you a bunch of business cards for people who install doors. They don't have any connection to the store, but the store knows that in order to sell doors you have to have somebody to install them, so the salesperson offers the installers' contact information to you as a courtesy. You take down a telephone number, call the installer, and ask him to come out. He may be qualified; more often, he's not. He puts in your door, and even though it may initially seem fine, problems soon develop. It won't close properly or sticks when you try to lock it. You go back to your home store and complain that the door isn't working, and can the store fix it?

But the home store salespeople tell you that it's not their problem and you have to contact your installer—and so begins the runaround. The installer (assuming he's willing and available to come back) will blame the door, the home store will blame the installer, the manufacturer will tell you it's not the manufacturer's problem, and you're back where you were with a nonworking door, minus quite a few dollars, not to mention the time wasted and the aggravation.

My father started our company when I was five years old and I was brought up with the sale of quality products. I heard these nightmarish stories from people all the time and decided that I wasn't going to run that kind of company. We buy products that are top of the line, we install them in a home, and when people call us, we're not going to give them the runaround. We buy it, we install it, and we service it. If customers call us, we go back out, see what's wrong, and take care of the problem—whatever we have to do to get the job done and done correctly. Make sure your door replacement company has the same policy. The home improvement industry is too much in the habit of pointing the finger at somebody else, and it counts on the fact that many customers will simply give up in frustration and hire someone else to fix whatever the original contractor messed up or, worse yet, live with the problem.

As far as warranties are concerned on a door, there's a plethora of things that can go wrong. If you don't paint your door according to the manufacturer's specifications, the warranty is voided. If you paint it after it's supposed to be painted, the warranty is voided. Most warranties are written to enable the manufacturers to wriggle out of them rather than to protect the consumer. The glass warranty on a door might be different than the slab warranty. Read your warranty carefully before you buy, because it may not be as solid as the salesperson tells you it is.

Even with our warranty, not every component is warranted equally. We have a 50-year warranty against warping, shrinking, swelling, and splitting, but the glass on our entry doors is guaranteed for 20 years against seal failures, plus three years on breakage for any reason. The hardware is covered for both mechanical and finishing defects for 50 years, plus 10 years on the finish. We have one of the best door warranties in the industry and it far exceeds anything you'd get from a box store, but as you see, it's still specific to the different components of the door.

There are a lot of good reasons to go with a full-service door company, and here's one I bet you never thought of: what your house is built on. Here's what we run into every now and then where people don't have their house built on a foundation but rather, on a slab or another less stable base: from winter to summer, houses not built on a solid foundation actually move a little bit, so if your door was installed in the summer, when it expands in the winter, it may not open or close properly. Also, if a door isn't installed right with the proper fastener on the top hinge, it will sag after a period of years and start hitting the frame. It's an easy thing to fix, but if it's done correctly in the first place, it won't need fixing.

With a custom door company like ours, you can get the style, the color, and the hardware color and configuration that you want, along with energy efficiency, durability, and installation that won't let you down. We have over 60 styles to choose from. I went through our brochure and counted 177 different options you can get for a door. Along with that, you can get 14 different colors. Add in to that all the varied types of glass packs available, and the possibilities are nearly endless.

What questions do you need to ask when you're shopping for a door? Number one, ask about the warranty, and don't be fooled if they tell you "it's good for a lifetime," as you'll sometimes be told at the big box home stores. People think, "Well, it's a lifetime so it's going to last forever," but ask the salesperson for a copy of the warranty and read through it before you buy. You'll be amazed at how little it actually covers.

Ask about service and installation, and what it covers: Does the company have an employee to install the door, so if you have a warranty issue, you can just call the company to fix it? Most of the time the company doesn't have such an employee. Ask too about the hardware options the store sells, and look carefully at what the guarantee covers and what it doesn't.

You'll need to find a reputable installer. References are your best bet here. Just because someone tells you that he's competent and experienced doesn't mean it's true. If a guy tells you he put in 150 doors last week, ask him, "Who'd you put them in for? I want to call them and see if you did a good job." Too often, people will ask for references but won't actually follow up on calling them. Don't be hesitant to follow up. I get a lot of calls from homeowners who want us to repair somebody else's shoddy work. I can't go do that and give them a warranty on someone else's work, because as soon as I touch it, I become the guy who's going to warranty it now, even though it's an inferior product.

The other question to ask when you're considering any home improvement company is whether the company specializes in that particular product. You never really get good at something unless you do it all the time. Our production crews install windows and doors—period. They don't install roofs or siding. Personally, I cringe when I see ads such as "XYZ Construction: roofing, siding, decks, windows, gutters and downspouts, building additions, garages." I can guarantee you that although the company may do all of those things, it doesn't do them all equally well. Go with a specialist, and you're much more likely to be satisfied with the results. A beautiful door says, "Welcome!" A well-made door saves you energy dollars and labor costs down the line, and a well-installed door works to keep you warm and secure in your home. If you're looking at new windows, do consider adding a new front door to complement the upgraded appearance your windows will give your home.

PATIO DOORS

Patio doors are a popular and attractive way to open up your home, and bring the outside in. Especially in a climate like ours, it's a way to enjoy the beauty of your yard despite the cold or heat outside. But patio doors, like any door, do wear out and need to be replaced. The good news is that new technology in building them has made them not just more attractive, but also far more energy efficient than in the past, which adds up to significant savings for you in fuel and electricity costs.

Let's talk a little about the varieties of patio door out there, and their relative plusses and minuses. We still see quite a few of the old-fashion aluminum sliders, especially in motels and places like that, but less frequently in homes. They're fairly unattractive and look dated, plus they're just not practical in our Wisconsin climate, because they frost up terribly and let a lot of cold in. It's difficult to keep wind from coming in around them, and to keep conduction through them to a minimum. In the summer, homeowners who have their dining set by the patio door may find that when the sun is out in the afternoon, or in the morning for that matter, they can't sit at the table because the heat will fry them. A lot of these old aluminum sliders don't slide, or slide with difficulty because the rollers are shot, or there's too much friction.

Security is a big issue with older patio doors too, because often you can walk up to one, lift the piece of glass right out of the frame, and walk into the house. Locks themselves are often substandard on these kinds of patio doors. I've seen a lot of people put a stick in the track to keep the door from being opened, and that's probably actually more effective than some of the locks you'll find on them. These doors are going the way of the dinosaurs, and that's a good thing.

Some homeowners look for wooden doors, strictly for the esthetics, but there isn't a wood patio door made that's genuinely energy efficient. It's the same conundrum that you run into looking at wood windows: even though the big companies make them, and some of them look nice, they're just not going to be as durable or as energy efficient. The problem is that the big companies have to compete on the price point with each other, which means that even at the top of the ready-made line, they're cutting corners to stay competitive. Even the best-known names in the business don't offer a triple-pane-glass pack at all, which is sad because as industry leaders, they could really do something for the green factor and saving energy. They don't have it because it costs more money to build a door that way, and they're afraid they're not going to get the sale if their product is more expensive than the competitor's.

Usually, the wooden sliders are not sold painted or stained. Typically, the outside is aluminum clad or vinyl clad, prefinished, and probably available in a variety of colors.

There are also solid vinyl doors available, and in the replacement-patio-door market, that's probably the one that people gravitate to the most often. A lot of companies manufacture vinyl doors, and they're cheap, cheaper than just about any other patio door out there, but they're the ones that come with the most problems with air infiltration and energy efficiency in long-term use. They just don't hold up. We used to sell high-end vinyl patio doors, but our experiences with them were not good, so we no longer do so.

Why is air or water infiltration the biggest problem with a typical patio door? Because there are so many moving parts on it, and so many nooks and crannies that air or water can get into, and the number of solutions are limited. Let's talk about water first. Say you've got a heavy rainstorm with wind blowing the rain against your patio door. That rain is running down the glass and going into the track of the patio door. Once it gets in that track, a weep system takes that water and "weeps" it back outside so it doesn't fill up the track and overflow into your home.

Most people don't know that system is on just about every patio door that's manufactured. If you don't have an effective weep system, you wind up with water inside the house. I actually heard about a guy who'd bought a competitor's vinyl patio door. His cat would drink water out of the sill of their sliding glass door as if it were a watering trough. And if you don't have an effective weep system—if water can get out—air can get in. Air will blow through the defective weep system and cause it to feel like a breeze coming in your home.

And make no mistake. Putting a patio door in is no job for the average Joe, no matter what they may tell you at the lumberyard. There's a lot that goes into getting the door to slide properly, and making sure it's 100 percent square and plumb, and all at the same time. That takes experience. Some friends of mine who had enough DIY experience to know better decided to replace their old slider themselves with a lumberyard sliding glass door. They didn't stint, and bought the top of the line. The guy who sold it to them assured them that it came with directions and shouldn't take more than a couple of hours to install, since according to the measurements they'd taken, it was an exact fit. Their first clue that his estimate might be off was the weight of the thing: over 250 pounds. Just getting it out of the car was a job. Three long, hot, frustrating (and potentially marriage-ending) days of hard labor later, they finally got it installed. Of course, the siding hasn't looked quite right since then, and some door parts were left over because they've never figured out what to do with them. But the door works. Mostly. Even I'm not immune to the do-it-yourself bug. I tried to install garage doors in my own home and, after two days, was more than happy to hand the job over to an expert who hung them in two hours. Never again!

Our patio doors are built especially for our Wisconsin climate, because energy efficiency here is paramount. We have a glass pack that's built for Wisconsin, with triple-pane glass and two coats of low-e. We also have the krypton gas between the panes, just as we have in the windows. When you're looking at a patio door and you see how much glass it contains, that's a significant amount of surface area, much more glass than frame. That's a big hole in the side of your home, and the potential for energy loss is tremendous if it's not built right, which is why we go to such lengths. Triple-paned patio doors aren't available at your big box store, or the lumberyard.

Our patio doors are made of composite so they're stronger than vinyl, and more energy efficient than wood. When you put the whole package together—the frame, and the glass, and all the components—it's a more energy-efficient patio door all around.

It's built to last because we have the 50-year warranty, just as we do on the windows and front doors. And that's a 50-year, non-prorated warranty because the whole door is guaranteed for 50 years, not some portion of it. People often ask me, "Why don't you guarantee it for a lifetime?" I ask them to be more specific. How long exactly do they think a "lifetime" is? They'll say, "Well, I don't know. It just lasts forever." But that's just not true. Again, as I discussed in chapter four when we asked the Wisconsin Bureau of Consumer protection to define what a "lifetime warranty" is, the following was their response. "If a window comes with a lifetime warranty the question is whose or what's lifetime—the lifetime of the company that manufactured the window, the lifetime of the installer, the lifetime of the purchaser, the lifetime of the window?" As you can see this is a very gray area. so be wary if someone offers you a lifetime warranty. Others might offer you what they call a "lifetime limited warranty." What does that mean? It means something's limited, and you won't know what that limit is until you actually read the warranty. Check it out for yourself. Go to your local lumberyard and actually read one—that is, if they have one at all. You get halfway down the first paragraph and there's already a proration schedule, which means if something goes wrong five years from now, they'll pay 50 percent, and the homeowner pays 50 percent. The burden is then on the consumer again. Personally, I just don't agree with that. It's not right. What that tells you is that they know they're not selling you a quality product at that point. It's something for which they're willing to go out on a limb for a couple years, but they're not willing to say it's guaranteed for 50 years, non-prorated, which should mean that in the forty-ninth year, if something goes wrong, it's still the manufacturer who covers 100 percent of it. That's why a non-prorated, 50-year warranty is the benchmark, as far as we're concerned. Others are too often not worth the paper they're printed on, but you don't find that out until something goes wrong. Of course, that kind of quality costs more, but what you get for your dollar is quality and service, without the dreaded runaround. Our customers get peace of mind, and that's why we're in business.

I once had a prospective customer tell me that she didn't care how often she had to replace her windows; she was happy just to go on vacation every 10 years, and have them redone. Most of us would find that logic inconvenient and expensive, if not downright absurd.

Some people don't care if it's a throw-away product. They'll just have it replaced and pay the money, and they don't care about energy efficiency because they've got enough money to pay the bills. That kind of thinking isn't typical, thank goodness, and given our legitimate concern about the environment, it's not even responsible. How do you know when it's time to replace your sliding glass doors? Here's a list of telltale problems:

- They don't open, or open only with difficulty.
- They don't lock, or the locking mechanisms are failing.
- The rollers or the sliding system are bad.
- You have wind and/or rain coming through.
- You're getting a lot of condensation in the wintertime, which is a sign of inefficiency.
- Your wooden patio door has rotted or stained wood (typically at the bottom where water seems to soak into the wood).
- You see moisture, spotting, clouding, or dirt between the panes, which is a sign of seal failure.

In our business, "seal failure" are dirty words because that's one of the biggest manufacturing problems with windows and doors that have glass in them. You want to keep that to a minimum in this business or you don't stay in this business, so working with a first class manufacturer is key. And seal failure is more than just an issue about how the glass looks; it indicates that it's not insulated glass anymore, so all the qualities that you had for insulation are gone. Now it's just two panes of glass.

A properly-made patio door has other qualities too, including the ability to reduce the kinds of harmful UV rays that can come into your home and damage and fade your carpets and upholstery. Our doors have three panes of glass. Two of the panes have a coat of low-e, or low emissivity, coating on them. When the sun hits the pane of glass from the outside, it reflects the ultraviolet rays back outside. To explain it more clearly, this coating is actually a very thin layer of metal. Some of it is titanium; some of it is silver oxide, and it reflects about 95 percent of those ultraviolet rays back outside.

It has a twofold purpose: When the sun is lower in the winter, it hits the glass at a lower angle, so it lets in the solar heat in winter. In summer, when the sun is higher in the sky, it reflects the heat out. Of course, because ours is built for Wisconsin, we have the best low-e, because there's a happy medium to be achieved when heat and sunlight are reflected out, and when we want them to come in. A Wisconsin homeowner wouldn't want a window made specifically for Florida, for instance, with the kind of low-e that they use there, because in Florida the concern is always to reflect the heat out. They don't care about solar heat gain in the winter because it's always warm. That's why the low-e used in the doors and windows in other climates is different than it is in Wisconsin. There's a happy medium to be achieved where you're cutting one off and not allowing the other one to work, and getting that specific result for our climate is the fruit of years of scientific research.

I'm an energy conservation freak, and I want the best for my customers in terms of quality, while at the same time, saving the greatest amount of energy that we possibly can for the environment. If you're paying winter fuel bills, you probably feel the same way. If you go to a big box store and are tempted by that good-looking, sliding patio door the store has for sale, it's important to remember the store is not making any adjustments for different climates, because the technology is expensive. Two coats of low-e costs more than one coat of low-e, and even the top-of-the-line, out-of-the-box manufacturers are only going to give you one coat.

There's a lot to know, and much of it very technical, when it comes to making the smart choice, but sadly, most people will base their choices on looks and price. If you go to a big box store, you're going to learn whatever that guy in aisle nine knows about window or door construction, and no more. It comes down to the price-versus-quality question so often. Yet, for most of us, our home is the biggest single investment we'll ever make; nothing else even comes close. Preserving and growing the value of your home as an investment needs to be taken into consideration when you're trying to choose between "good" and "good enough."

When you come to think of it, a lot of people out there are paying for the windows; they just don't have them in their houses. What I mean by that is this: When you buy energy-efficient windows, and you put them in today and sell your house tomorrow, you get 75 percent back in resale value alone. You take into account the energy efficiency and how much you're going to save on energy, and that adds up to quite a bit. Additionally, with new windows, you don't have any maintenance. You don't have to scrape, paint, or do any other kind of maintenance ever again. When you add those savings together, you can understand why I say that a lot of people are paying for good windows; they just don't have them installed.

We do a lot of home shows. I don't attend as many as I used to, but I remember how, usually, people would come through, stop at our booth, and talk about windows or patio doors. I would show them what I had to offer. A lot of what I'd talk about would be about our service, our company, and how we take care of our customers. Then I'd go out and give them an estimate, and they would ultimately go with a different product or a different company. Of course, I didn't hold it against them, because I had my chance. I showed them my product, and made my case. If they didn't want it, well, I had done my best. Then, the next time I'd see them at a home show, I'd ask them how it had gone for them. Sometimes they'd say, "Well, we didn't do anything," which for me is actually nice to hear, because that means I still have the opportunity to work with them. All too often, however, I'd hear a version of this: " I wish we'd just have gone with you guys because this other guy came over and gave us a lower estimate, so we ordered windows from him. About three months later, we finally got them. Then they sent some guy out to try and put them in, but he wasn't experienced at doing that kind of a window …" The nightmare stories just keep coming, all a little bit different but essentially all the same.

I hate hearing that, because I don't feel I did my job at that point. It's not as if I didn't warn them, either. They shared their story because I told them what might happen. Why do folks make the wrong choice? Because they confused price with value.

Everybody wants to save a dime, and I understand that. I'm the same way. At the same time, at least look at the value you're getting for the dime you're spending and evaluate it. Spending more doesn't mean spending more money and getting the same value. In fact, if you were to choose the most expensive thing in any category and buy it, you'd almost certainly wind up happier with what you had than if you'd bought the lowest-priced thing in that category.

The bottom line? Quality may cost you more upfront, but the savings show up over the long term, not at the point of purchase. In the case of windows and doors, the savings show up in fuel costs, ease of operation and maintenance, and guaranteed service. Windows and doors are a long-lasting, long-term investment or, at least, they should be! Don't make the mistake of confusing low price with good value; it almost never is.

KEEP IN MIND:

- Given the amount of glass in a patio door, it can be a big source of energy loss if it's not properly made and installed.

- A typical glass "slider" is a potential home security risk, since the locking mechanisms are nearly always below par.

- Not all patio doors are created equal, and what's right for a Florida climate is not the same thing you need in Wisconsin.

CHAPTER NINE

OUTRO

W hen it comes to replacing your home's windows and doors, we know that you have many choices. We've been taking good care of our neighbors from Green Bay to Oshkosh, Neenah to Wausau, Madison to Beaver Dam, Reedsburg to White-water, and everywhere in between, since 1967. That makes us one of the most experienced Wisconsin replacement window contractors, and for good reason. We've absolutely delighted more than 12,000 and counting homeowners with our warm and welcoming approach to doing business.

Our goal from the very start of the company has been to offer consumers the best value for their money. Many times the children of previous customers call to have us install our windows or doors in their first homes after witnessing the value their parents received from our company. We are in the business for the long run, intent on bringing value to generation after generation. Much of our success is due to the fact that we're from right here. We understand Wisconsin weather and Wisconsin folks. We all grew up around here and our staff and their families are part of the community. We treat every job as if we were doing the work for neighbors because we *are* doing the work for neighbors!

Some window companies offer a manufacturer warranty on window parts. AHT Wisconsin Windows is one of the few replacement window companies in Wisconsin to offer a full 50-year, nonprorated warranty on our windows. The warranty is not prorated and is fully transferable if you sell your home. No worries with us! AHT Wisconsin Windows is a licensed contractor in the state of Wisconsin, and we carry full liability and workers' compensation insurance coverage for every job.

In addition we are fully certified by the manufacturers of the windows and doors that we install. Because we are certified, all manufacturer warranties are valid and in full effect.

Installation by a noncertified contractor may mean that the warranty is invalid.

People other than our customers think we are okay too. AHT Wisconsin Windows has been named one of *Qualified Remodeler* magazine's top 500 home improvement companies every year since 1998. Our company has also been ranked in *Remodeling* magazine's Top 550 listing and *Replacement Contractor* magazine's Replacement 100 list, in addition to our Guild Quality award with distinction for customer satisfaction and our A+ rating with the Better Business Bureau. The Wisconsin Division of Safety and Buildings certifies us as a financially responsible contractor. We're a member of the Valley Home Builders Association, and a member of MABA (Madison Area Builders Association). Our products are American made, and all of our installers are employees who've been certified to install our products.

If you have any questions we didn't answer in this book, feel free to calls us toll-free at (800) 387-9450, or visit our websites at www.ahtwindows.com, or wwww.scottthewindowguy.com There's a lot of information there that will help you make informed choices no matter where you are or whom you choose to work with.

KNOW YOUR WINDOW TERMS

When replacing the windows in your Wisconsin home, you may be faced with a number of terms and phrases that are unfamiliar. Here are some terms you should know in order to make a more informed decision when discussing new windows with your Wisconsin replacement window contractor.

Air Infiltration: Air coming through the window around the sash, meeting rail or other places that allow air to infiltrate into the home.

Bay window: A composite of three or more windows, usually made up of a large center unit and two flanking units at 30°, 45° or 90° angles to the wall.

Bow window: A composite of four or more window units in a radial or bow formation.

Brick mold: Outside casing around window to cover jambs and through which nails are driven to install the window.

Casing: Inside casing is a flat, decorative molding that covers the inside edge of the jambs and the rough openings between the window unit and the wall. Outside casing (or brick mold) serves the same purpose, while it also is an installation device through which nails are driven to install the window unit to the wall.

Condensation: Moisture that forms on the glass or frame of a window or door.

Conduction: Cold or heat transfer through the glass or frame of a window or door.

Double-glazing: Use of two panes of glass in a window to increase energy efficiency and provide other performance benefits.

Drip cap: A molding placed on the top of the head brick mold or casing of a window frame.

Fenestration: An architectural term referring to the arrangement of windows in a wall.

Glazing: The glass panes or lights in a sash of a window.

Glazing bead: A plastic or wood strip applied to the window sash around the perimeter of the glass.

Header: A heavy beam extended across the top of the rough opening to prevent the weight of the wall from resting on the window frame.

Lite (also spelled light): Glazing framed by a sash in a window or door.

Low-e glass: A common term used to refer to glass that has low emissivity due to a film or metallic coating on the glass or suspended between the two panes of glass to restrict the passage of radiant heat.

Mullion: The vertical or horizontal divisions or joints between single windows in a multiple window unit.

Rough opening: The opening left in a frame wall to receive a window unit.

Sash balance: A system of weight, cords, and/or coiled springs that assist in raising a double-hung sash and tend to keep the sash in any placed position by counterbalancing the weight of the sash.

Sash cord: In double-hung windows, the rope or chain that attaches the sash to the counter balance.

Sash weights: In older double-hung windows, the concealed cast-iron weights that are used to counterbalance the sash.

Shims: Wood wedges (often wood shingles) used to secure the window unit in a rough or masonry opening in a square, level, and plumb position during and after installation.

Side lights: Tall, narrow, fixed sashes on either or both sides of a door to light an entryway or vestibule.

Sill: Horizontal member that forms the bottom of a window frame.

Single glazing: Use of single panes of glass in a window. Not as energy-efficient as double-glazing or triple-glazing.

Single-hung: A single-hung type of window in which the top sash is fixed or inoperable.

Stud: Vertical wood framing members that form a frame wall. In normal construction these are eight-feet-long 2 x 4s.

Transom: A smaller window above a door or another window. A transom joint is also the horizontal joining area between two window units that are stacked one on top of the other.

Triple-glazing: A sash glazed with three lights of glass, enclosing two separate air spaces.

U-factor: A measure of heat transmission through a wall or window. The lower the U-factor, the better the insulating value.

Windowpane divider: A short bar used to separate glass in a sash into multiple lights. Also called a grille.

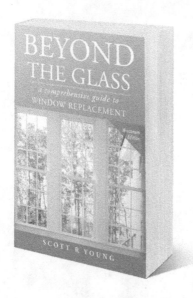

How can you use this book?

MOTIVATE

EDUCATE

THANK

INSPIRE

PROMOTE

CONNECT

Why have a custom version of *Beyond the Glass*?

- Build personal bonds with customers, prospects, employees, donors, and key constituencies
- Develop a long-lasting reminder of your event, milestone, or celebration
- Provide a keepsake that inspires change in behavior and change in lives
- Deliver the ultimate "thank you" gift that remains on coffee tables and bookshelves
- Generate the "wow" factor

Books are thoughtful gifts that provide a genuine sentiment that other promotional items cannot express. They promote employee discussions and interaction, reinforce an event's meaning or location, and they make a lasting impression. Use your book to say "Thank You" and show people that you care.

Beyond the Glass is available in bulk quantities and in customized versions at special discounts for corporate, institutional, and educational purposes. To learn more please contact our Special Sales team at:

1.866.775.1696 • sales@advantageww.com • www.AdvantageSpecialSales.com

9 781599 324166